MEASURING AND MANAGING KNOWLEDGE

Thomas Housel, Ph.D.
Arthur H. Bell, Ph.D.

McGraw-Hill Irwin

Boston   Burr Ridge, IL   Dubuque, IA   Madison, WI   New York   San Francisco   St. Louis
Bangkok   Bogotá   Caracas   Kuala Lumpur   Lisbon   London   Madrid   Mexico City
Milan   Montreal   New Delhi   Santiago   Seoul   Singapore   Sydney   Taipei   Toronto

Dedication

Tom Housel dedicates this work to his parents who made sure that he was put in early school environments that made acquiring new knowledge a pure delight and to Father Evan R. Williams who created that delight in learning at the Christ Church Episcopal Day School.

Art Bell dedicates this work to his mother, Dorothy, for whom knowledge has always been a delight.

McGraw-Hill Higher Education ⚡
*A Division of The **McGraw-Hill** Companies*

MEASURING AND MANAGING KNOWLEDGE

Published by McGraw-Hill/Irwin, an imprint of The McGraw-Hill Companies, Inc., 1221 Avenue of the Americas, New York, NY, 10020. Copyright © 2001, by The McGraw-Hill Companies, Inc. All rights reserved. No part of this publication may be reproduced or distributed in any form or by any means, or stored in a data base or retrieval system, without the prior written consent of The McGraw-Hill Companies, Inc., including, but not limited to, in any network or other electronic storage or transmission, or broadcast for distance learning. Some ancillaries, including electronic and print components, may not be available to customers outside the United States.

This book is printed on acid-free paper.

1 2 3 4 5 6 7 8 9 0   DOC/DOC   0 9 8 7 6 5 4 3 2 1

ISBN 0-07-229771-9

Publisher: *George Werthman*
Sponsoring editor: *Rick Williamson*
Senior marketing manager: *Jeffrey Parr*
Associate project manager: *Destiny Rynne*
Senior production supervisor: *Michael R. McCormick*
Freelance design coordinator: *Mary L. Christianson*
Cover design: *The Davis Group*
Interior design: *PhotoDisc*
Senior supplement coordinator: *Marc Mattson*
New media: *David Barrick*
Compositor: Lachina Publishing Services
Typeface: 10/12 Times Roman
Printer: *R. R. Donnelley & Sons Company*

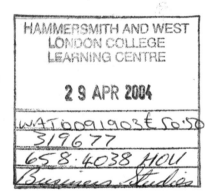

Library of Congress Cataloging-in-Publication Data

Housel, Thomas J.
  Measuring and managing knowledge / by Thomas Housel and Arthur H. Bell
    p. cm.
  Includes index.
  ISBN 0-07-229771-9 (alk. paper)
  1. Knowledge management.   I. Bell, Arthur H. (Arthur Henry), 1946–   II. Title.
HD30.2.H677 2001
658.4'038--dc21   2001018714

www.mhhe.com

319677

BRIEF CONTENTS

	FOREWORD	ix
	PREFACE	xi
	INTRODUCTION	xiii
Chapter 1	The Parameters of Knowledge Management	1
Chapter 2	The Knowledge-Based Economy	15
Chapter 3	Paradigms for Knowledge Management	29
Chapter 4	Knowledge Management Principles	45
Chapter 5	Knowledge Management at Work in Organizations	63
Chapter 6	Knowledge Measurement and Value	77
Chapter 7	Measuring Return on Knowledge	91
Chapter 8	Electronic Tools for Managing Knowledge	109
Chapter 9	Implementing Knowledge Management	127
Chapter 10	The Future of Knowledge Management	143
Appendix	Annotated Bibliography	155
	INDEX	159

CONTENTS

FORWARD ix

PREFACE xi

INTRODUCTION xiii

Chapter 1 The Parameters of Knowledge Management 1

WHAT CAN HAPPEN TO KNOWLEDGE 4
    Knowledge Can Be Born 4
    Knowledge Can Die 5
    Knowledge Can Be Owned 7
    Knowledge Is Immanent as Well as Extant 9
    Knowledge Can Be Stored 9
KNOWLEDGE CAN BE CATEGORIZED 10
CONCLUSION 12
QUESTIONS FOR REVIEW 13
CASE STUDY: BIG BRANDS FOODS, INC.: A KNOWLEDGE MANAGEMENT CASE 13

Chapter 2 The Knowledge-Based Economy 15

PRODUCTS AND SERVICES 15
CHALLENGES AND OPPORTUNITIES 16
ECONOMY IN TRANSITION 17
    Brave New World 18
    The Global Brave New World 18
KNOWLEDGE-BASED ECONOMIES 20
    Impact of the Knowledge Economy 21
    Knowledge Capital 21
    Value vs. Cost of Knowledge Assets 23

	Intangible vs. Tangible Assets	23
	The Knowledge Organization in the New Economy	23
	CONCLUSION	26
	QUESTIONS FOR REVIEW	26
	CASE STUDY: DELL AND THE INTERNET	27
Chapter 3	**Paradigms for Knowledge Management**	**29**
	Fundamental Assumptions	29
	MEASUREMENT IS ESSENTIAL TO MANAGEMENT	32
	Process of Elimination	33
	It's in Here Somewhere	34
	Everything Is Cost	37
	Rorschach Inkblot	38
	Outputs Focus	39
	Knowledge Is Proportionate to Value	39
	CONCLUSION	42
	QUESTIONS FOR REVIEW	42
	CASE STUDY: HUGHES SPACE AND COMMUNICATIONS	43
Chapter 4	**Knowledge Management Principles**	**45**
	KNOWLEDGE MANAGEMENT OVERVIEW	46
	KNOWLEDGE MANAGEMENT AND VALUE CREATION	47
	THE STATE OF KNOWLEDGE MANAGEMENT	48
	WHY IS KNOWLEDGE MANAGEMENT IMPORTANT?	49
	PRACTICAL PRINCIPLES FOR MANAGING KNOWLEDGE	50
	Customer Knowledge	50
	Knowledge and IT	55
	Monitoring and Measuring Knowledge	57
	CONCLUSION	60
	QUESTIONS FOR REVIEW	60
	CASE STUDY: THE DISTANCE LEARNING CASE	61
Chapter 5	**Knowledge Management at Work in Organizations**	**63**
	KNOWLEDGE MANAGEMENT IN PRACTICE	63
	Dow Chemical	65
	The World Bank	67
	Skandia	67
	Hewlett-Packard	68
	Core Competencies at Chase Manhattan and Canadian Imperial Bank of Commerce	68
	Chevron	69
	Chaparral Steel	69
	Knowledge Networking at British Petroleum (BP)	69
	Monsanto	70
	More Current Applications	70

	CONCLUSION	74
	QUESTIONS FOR REVIEW	75
	CASE STUDY: THE UNITED RADIOLOGY CASE	75

Chapter 6	Knowledge Measurement and Value	77
	EXPONENTIAL GROWTH PHASE OF THE KNOWLEDGE ECONOMY	78
	THREATS TO EXPONENTIAL GROWTH AND HOW KNOWLEDGE	
	METRICS WILL HELP	79
	First	79
	Second	79
	Third	79
	The Bottom Line	80
	THE CONSUMER AND KNOWLEDGE METRICS: REDEFINING THE	
	PRODUCT/SERVICE	80
	THE INVESTOR AND KNOWLEDGE METRICS: MEASUREMENT OF	
	RETURNS AT ALL LEVELS	81
	MANAGEMENT AND KNOWLEDGE METRICS: TRANSFORMING	
	KNOWLEDGE INTO VALUE	82
	TRADITIONAL VALUATION METHODOLOGIES VIS-À-VIS KNOWLEDGE METRICS	82
	COST, INCOME, MARKET, AND REAL OPTIONS APPROACHES	83
	CONCLUSION	86
	QUESTIONS FOR REVIEW	87
	CASE STUDY: DECISIONS AT MCKESSON	87

Chapter 7	Measuring Return on Knowledge	91
	KNOWLEDGE-VALUE-ADDED METHODOLOGY	91
	KVA Example	92
	KVA Theory	93
	KVA: EXODUS COMMUNICATIONS INC.	95
	Company Description	96
	Current Issues	97
	Aggregate-Level KVA	97
	KVA: Sales Provisioning Process	102
	CONCLUSION	106
	QUESTIONS FOR REVIEW	106

Chapter 8	Electronic Tools for Knowledge Management	109
	SCOPING THE PROBLEM	109
	What Is Knowledge?	110
	Infrastructure vs. Services	110
	Computational Tools	110
	KSS: KNOWLEDGE STRUCTURE AND SERVICES	111
	Knowledge Structure	111
	Knowledge Services	112
	Infrastructure Services	113

Core Services   114
Packaged Services   116
The Knowledge Structure and Services (KSS) Matrix and the
    KSS Checklist   117
USING THE KSS MATRIX AND CHECKLIST TO COMPARE CURRENT
    KNOWLEDGE MANAGEMENT TOOLS   118
Documentum 4i   118
OpenText LiveLink   119
Autonomy KnowledgeServer   119
Lotus Notes R5   120
PeopleSoft Customer Relationship Management   121
CONCLUSION   121
QUESTIONS FOR REVIEW   122
CASE STUDY: THE INFORMEDIA DIGITAL LIBRARY PROJECT   123

Chapter 9   Implementing Knowledge Management   127

"Electronic Propinquity"   128
Shifting the Paradigm   128
Knowledge Asset Portfolio   129
Gaps in Knowledge Asset Portfolios   130
Designing Knowledge-Based Implementations   131
TO DEEPEN ANALYSIS   134
The Knowledge Management Maturity Model   136
Managing Customer Relationship and Supply Chain Knowledge   137
CONCLUSION   141
QUESTIONS FOR REVIEW   142
EXERCISE: DEVELOP A KNOWLEDGE STRATEGY   142

Chapter 10   The Future of Knowledge Management   143

THE ERA OF EMBEDDED KNOWLEDGE   144
OMNIPRESENT EMBEDDING   145
THE "KNOWING" RELATIONSHIP   145
CHOICES: UNEMBEDDED OR EMBEDDED KNOWLEDGE   146
THE BIRTH AND DEATH OF PARADIGMS   147
TECHNOLOGY AND EMBEDDED KNOWLEDGE   148
BEYOND NATURE: THE EMBEDDED ENVIRONMENT   149
LIVING IN THE TECHNOLOGICAL FOREST   149
FREEDOM AND META-KNOWLEDGE   150
THE AGE OF META-KNOWLEDGE MANAGEMENT   151
CONCLUSION   153
QUESTIONS FOR REVIEW   153

Appendix   Annotated Bibliography   155

INDEX   159

FOREWORD

We have had several centuries to adjust to the idea of managing people and measuring their skills. No doubt the first administrators and executives found this a thorny, intractable task indeed. We have also had a similar span of time to come to terms with managing and measuring money, and accountancy too must have seemed an overwhelming endeavor for the original bean-counters.

A new, similarly enormous challenge is now at hand. Within the last decade we have taken seriously the art and science of measuring and managing knowledge. Like the earliest administrators and accountants, we cannot help but feel the difficulty and complexity of the task. At the same time, the case for the necessity of such measurement and management is clear. Modern organizations thrive to the extent that they gather, nurture, apply, protect, and refresh their stores of knowledge about markets, product development, deployment of resources, business processes, and host of other practical business concerns.

Housel and Bell are pioneers and chroniclers in the endeavor of managing and measuring knowledge. In these chapters, they set forth one of the crucial first maps of the intellectual territory to be explored and understood. Beginning with useful working definitions and descriptions of knowledge per se, they summarize main routes of inquiry to date and blaze several new trails of their own (especially in their discussion of the Knowledge Value-Added approach to knowledge measurement and their prophetic view of what lies ahead for knowledge management). At every turn, they support their argument and analysis with the pertinent, timely business details and examples. The cases that punctuate their book give the reader the opportunity to participate in the mind-stretching adventure of discovery and application. Their tools for investigating approaches and applications for knowledge measurement and management are selected with the manager or management student in mind.

The authors of this book are the first to admit, as they do explicitly in several chapters, that many paths and tributaries of knowledge management are as yet unmapped, and sometimes unimagined. But they make the case powerfully that the measurement and management of knowledge in the new century is of comparable importance to the measurement and management of people and money in the past. As in those latter fields, we have before us not an interesting island of inquiry but instead a continent-sized topic, both in its implications for business and life.

Warren Bennis
University Professor and Distinguished Professor of Business Administration
Marshall School of Business University of Southern California
and
Author of a new book entitled *Geeks and Geezers*

PREFACE

At the dawn of a new century, the principal assets of many (perhaps most) corporations are now held in the intangible form of intellectual capital. The primary market value of Microsoft, for example, lies not in its buildings, equipment, or receivables, but instead in the smarts of its people, software development capacity, patents, copyrights, and trademarks.

This book provides a framework for managing and maximizing the return on knowledge assets. Like any emerging field, knowledge management has so far been hobbled by a lack of clarity on key questions: What do we mean by "knowledge"? How can it be measured and managed? How can return on knowledge be maximized? To answer these questions, the authors avoid the obtuse language of sociology and economics in favor of plain talk. They weave the central insights of the growing body of knowledge management literature and their own research into a clear, compelling story of what knowledge management is at present and will become in the years ahead.

Managing and Measuring Knowledge teaches through the case method, with extended discussion and investigation of high-interest business scenarios from the areas of health management, investment, the Internet, telecommunications, computer technologies, food industry management, heavy industry, and a variety of service industries. In each case, readers learn how new tools of knowledge management can positively impact bottom-line profits and overall business strategy. Readers conclude that businesses in a knowledge economy achieve competitive advantage by the thoroughness, creativity, and insight with which they manage and measure their knowledge assets.

ACKNOWLEDGMENTS

This traditional portion of front matter has special significance in a book on knowledge management. Acknowledgments give the authors, individually and together, an opportunity to reflect on the many streams and sources of knowledge that have been influential on this work and for which they are profoundly grateful. For Tom Housel, thanks go to Sandra Hom for her major contribution to Chapter 2, Dick Chase for his guidance and contributions in Chapter 4, Richard Bergin for his unique and very insightful contributions on customer interface knowledge, Verna Allee for her very constructive suggestions and material in Chapter 9, Sarah Nelson for her extensive editing and contributions to Chapter 6, Alicia Moani DeLoach for her hard work and contributions to the cases in Chapter 5, Dr. Waymond Rodgers for his help with accounting issues, Eliza Chen for her help with the Chapter 7 Exodus case study, Roger Yao for his help with Chapter 9, and the IOM department staff and work study students for their help in making sure the manuscript made it from my desk to the editor (no small feat in and of itself). Love and special thanks go to wife Mary Housel for her careful and detailed editing of the manuscript and to son Christopher for letting Daddy work when he really should have been playing with his son.

For Art Bell, thanks go to colleagues who have shared their insights and intelligence not only in their publications and research but in stimulating conversation: Dean Gary Williams and Associate Deans Denis Neilson, Eugene Muscat, and Sal Aceves of the School of Business and Management, University of San Francisco; Professors Karl Boedecker, Dan Blakley, Steve Alter, Oren Harari, Nick Imparato, Jonathan Barsky, Zhan Li, Roger Chen, Peggy Takahashi, Carol Graham, Mark Cannice, Les Myers, Ofelia Alayeto, Heather Cowan-Spiegel, Norman Sigband, Rex Bennett, Alev Efendioglu, Kathy Kane, Bill Murray, Steven Huxley, Manuel Tarrazzo, and Rich Puntillo. Thanks is also extended to friends in business and industry, including Robert Bell, Hinda Smith, Gary Weatherford, Stacey Remington, Tom Duffy, Bob and Chris Miller, Matt and Roberta Masson, Steve and Susan Machtinger, Joe and Mary Vella, Larry and Simone Jordan, and Reverend Walter Bouman. Art sends special thanks and love to his wife Dayle, son Art, and daughters Lauren and Madeleine.

INTRODUCTION

The last decade has seen the birth of a new science—knowledge management. Its long, ongoing infancy is accompanied by all the expected frustrations of growth and development. This fledgling science struggles to be more sure of its steps, more in control of its forward motion, and more certain in its judgments and communications. While dot-coms made the headlines (and, more recently, the financial obituaries), the quieter child of the new century made steady progress in helping both New and Old Economy companies understand the nature of their knowledge assets and, by extension, the necessity to nurture and shepherd those assets wisely.

For many companies, the new science of knowledge management has arrived as an *enfant terrible.* These companies, deeply invested both literally and figuratively in old assumptions, found the implications of knowledge management puzzling at best and nonsensical at worst. Employees could be managed, but how could those tools be applied to knowledge itself? Dollars could be measured and tracked, but how could established accounting procedures measure knowledge?

The simple answer to these questions is, they can't. Old Economy management and measurement tools are inadequate or largely irrelevant to the emerging new paradigm of knowledge management. By analogy, the zodiac and other ancient tools for finding constellations in the sky have little or no usefulness for scientific observation of the stars and planets. But companies have understandable difficulty leaving the sunset world of old assumptions for the darker, lesser known region of pre-dawn, with only the slightest glimmers of new light to guide them. Living within the comfort of an accepted business paradigm prevents most companies from peeking over the fence to observe, in Yeats's words, "what rough beast slouches toward Bethlehem to be born." The comfort of what one believes and accepts evaporates quickly under the harsh light of new and perhaps more true ideas and perspectives. For example, imagine the internal confusion and consternation in an Old Economy company that had "managed" employees on the basis of seniority rather than on their contribution to the intellectual capital of the enterprise. Imagine the regret of such a company when a major layoff was undertaken without consideration for the core knowledge exiting the company, pink slip in hand.

This book targets companies and managers who are prepared to be uncomfortable with old assumptions. We recognize that this is a time not for final chapters on the new science of knowledge management but instead a time for explorative essays that frame important questions. The potential enlightenment of a dramatic new paradigm for business begins by turning on a few lights. Chapter by chapter, this book asks the reader to sustain the discomfort of competing paradigms as the vision of new patterns and processes clashes with and begins to crowd out older, more established views.

1

THE PARAMETERS
OF KNOWLEDGE
MANAGEMENT

The decades of the last century saw corporations locked in a struggle to out-*do* one another. The 21st century will pit corporations in a struggle to out-*know* one another.

Making the transition from *doing* to *knowing* in business, from capacity of effort to capacity of insight, is both challenging and hazardous. More than half of the companies listed as members of the Fortune 500 in 1993 are not on that list today. Even icon names such as McDonald's and Sears find themselves in a slump. "What are we *doing* wrong?" ask corporate leaders and shareholders. They don't *know,* because attention to knowing—in effect, knowledge management—is a new idea for most companies. They are comfortable discussing the management of people, products, financial resources, and operations. They are not comfortable discussing the management of knowledge.

This book intends to increase that comfort level with knowledge management across industries. The opening chapter will serve as a walking tour of the broad and sometimes uncharted territory suggested by the concept "knowledge management." To "manage" something, after all, presumes that one has *defined* what is to be managed. In the case of stock portfolio management, for example, what one does as a manager depends directly upon the definition, nature, and contents of the stock portfolio at hand. *Knowing* one's stock portfolio is not an overwhelming intellectual endeavor.

But "knowing" what knowledge to manage is a significant intellectual challenge. Specifying the definition, nature, and contents of "knowledge" itself can be daunting, even if one restricts the pursuit solely to knowledge applicable to business. Significantly, in the new economy, business knowledge is an expansive concept, embracing not only traditional areas such as economics and finance but also the "hard" sciences in all branches, including computer science, applied technologies, decision systems, sociology, psychology, rhetoric, and persuasion theory. To a previously unrealized degree, philosophy and religion have a part to play.

Let us begin, therefore, with a general and commonsense definition of "knowledge." This definition serves as a starting point for our survey of the ground to be covered, and will be refined, qualified, and to some degree challenged by subsequent chapters in this book.

Knowledge is an ideational (i.e., conceptual rather than physical) construct generated through the agency of the human mind.

The broad terms of this definition make it possible to include all the following aspects of knowledge in our consideration:

- Seemingly important and unimportant thoughts. One's philosophy of government and one's shoe size are both forms of knowledge. The definition of knowledge is not constrained by *valuation* or *relative usefulness.*
- "Proven" as well as unproven or unprovable ideas. The apparent certainty of human mortality or the hydrogen-oxygen bond comprising water is knowledge, but no more so than notions regarding human immortality or speculations about time travel. The definition of knowledge is not constrained by systems of *logic* or *proof.*
- Morally approved and morally disapproved ideas. The thoughts of Mother Teresa and those of Hitler are both forms of knowledge. The definition of knowledge is not constrained by *moral philosophies.*
- Individually or widely held ideas. An item of information possessed by only one research scientist in the world is knowledge; information held by virtually every adult on the planet is also knowledge. The definition of knowledge is not constrained by its *relative distribution.*
- Beliefs, attitudes, speculations, predispositions, lifestyle choices, and habits of mind that are a composite of rational and irrational or emotional elements. One's disinclination to eat meat containing growth hormones is a form of knowledge. Blushing (i.e., the experience of emotion), by contrast, is not a form of knowledge; the thoughts that give rise to blushing are a form of knowledge. The definition of knowledge is not constrained by an *admixture of nonrational components.*
- Ideas actively held within the human mind as well as ideas given tangible form through writing or electromechanical records outside the human mind. One's idea on a given Tuesday for a delectable lunch is knowledge, but so is the menu composed by a restaurateur 20 years ago and now no longer consciously held in any human mind. The definition of knowledge is not constrained by the *locus* or *form* of ideas.
- Ideational constructs produced by agency of the human mind but now existing in a way that cannot be held in mind or manipulated by ordinary thought. The complex bit patterns flashing through the central processing unit of a computer are forms of "artificial" knowledge with their genesis in human thought. They exist in a form within the computer that is not conducive to active mental conceptualization or manipulation by the human mind. The definition of knowledge is not constrained by the ability of the human mind to *conceive* or *perceive* the knowledge forms to which it has given birth.

With this working definition of knowledge as our initial guide, let's experiment briefly with three illustrative cases:

1. The idea-versus-thing dilemma. A physical, living, breathing cow as it stands in the pasture is not in itself knowledge. Managing knowledge is not the same as managing things. Companies make this mistake when, in an effort to manage knowledge within the organization, they end up creating management structures for things and people. Take, for example, the policy statement "All capital expenditures must be approved by the CFO." That policy, in itself, does not manage knowledge (the knowledge, for example, possessed by the CFO that allows wise decision making). Instead, the policy confuses knowledge with entities such as the CFO position.

   Artificial intelligence in its many forms may be thought of knowledge also. In a business context, there is no "knower," and hence no knowledge, apart from the human participants in the business enterprise. Knowledge does not hover disembodied in company tradition ("the way we operate around here"), policy manuals (only ink and paper apart from human cognition), or complex assembly or distribution systems. If a company wants to *know* what it is doing, both the questions and the answers will come through human intellectual effort, however assisted by machines, and scaled to human needs and perspectives.

2. The involvement of the human mind. What a fly actually perceives as it looks through its multidimensional eyes at a flower is not knowledge, at least as far as we humans are concerned. We cannot know as the fly knows, if *knowing* can even be used meaningfully with regard to the fly. But our theories or models of the nature of that alien form of fly vision *are* forms of knowledge. In other words, the generation of knowledge must have originally involved *human cognition* in some way.

3. The time-bound nature of knowledge. What we see as stars in the night sky are not "there"; in most cases, we are viewing the light sent out by those stars hundreds or thousands of light-years ago. We are literally seeing where they used to be. Whether they exist "now" is so far unknowable. Some forms of knowledge are limited by the space/time event horizon. Notice, however, that we can "know" that we do *not* know the physical state of objects such as stars apart from their perceived space/time flow of information in the form of light. Knowledge of this sort is not constrained by the event horizon. For example, if the sun were to suddenly explode, we would not "know" about the explosion for the eight minutes it takes for light to travel to us from the sun. To that extent, our knowledge is limited by the event horizon. Yet we know that we are inevitably eight minutes "late" in perceiving events taking place on the sun. This knowledge is not bound by time or space.

Put in business terms, our efforts to know are often bedeviled by a time lag. In hiring a new manager, for example, you may have a fulsome record of where he or she *was* based on a résumé and references. But where he or she *is* at present, in terms of what knowledge and abilities they now bring to your business, can be a different matter entirely, as too many employers discover to their disappointment. Historical knowledge is not contemporary or predictive knowledge. Hence, managing knowledge must pay attention to more than past knowledge.

WHAT CAN HAPPEN TO KNOWLEDGE

Our walking tour of the general landscape of knowledge management can be arranged as visits to various locations where knowledge is generated or changes in some way. By apprising ourselves of the influences and transformations to which knowledge is subject, we set the stage for an eventual inclusive framework by which to manage knowledge.

Knowledge Can Be Born

What apparently distinguishes *Homo sapiens* from the rest of the animal world is our ability to conceive, store, and manipulate ideas linguistically apart from the stimuli that gave rise to them. We can think about and name apples—make recipes for their use, use their visual image for decoration, even name computers after them—without being under the influence of the smell, taste, feel, and appearance of actual apples. We can give birth to ideas as well as manipulate and change them.

Certainly every company desires such intellectual fertility on the part of its employees, particularly its leaders. But what are the circumstances that prove most conducive to the birth of new knowledge? Which individuals are most fertile in their ability to generate new knowledge? Why these individuals and not others? How can these individuals be discovered and nurtured? These are questions asked by organizations and human enterprises of all kinds. Organizations crave knowledge spawners much as living organisms crave reproductive opportunities and capabilities. In both cases, the motive is the same: survival and maximization of life experience. The latter phrase, admittedly vague, may involve fulfillment through growth, perceptual satisfaction (pleasures of the senses), increased security during stasis ("a chicken in every pot"), or accomplishments (mission achievement, etc.).

Knowledge spawners equip their organizations to confront change successfully. For example, rapidly changing global markets can threaten the viability of even the most established businesses. These companies rely upon new knowledge to maintain and extend their markets. The companies' highly valued knowledge spawners come up with the biomedical formula, the algorithm for a faster chip, the alloy for a lighter autobody, or the economic model for a better deployment of resources that allow their organizations to thrive when others are failing.

Increasingly, the spawning of knowledge involves a partnership between human cognition and machine-based intelligence. When a pharmaceutical company conducts a complex series of drug tests by means of computer analysis; when a physician makes a diagnosis based primarily on output from an expert system; when an aeronautics corporation designs an aircraft from computer-based flight test data, the question of where requisite knowledge resides for these tasks is not easily answered. On one hand, human project designers and data interpreters are certainly important knowledge sources. On the other hand, computers or other systems generate substantial and significant knowledge. Traditionally based on human inputs, this artificial knowledge is increasingly self-generated by artificial intelligence capabilities.

Any plan for knowledge management must make provision for both direct human knowledge and indirect human knowledge, as mediated by machines, which extend and enhance the powers of mind.

Knowledge Can Die

In terms of sheer quantity, the vast majority of things known by human beings die with them. Few of us record even one-thousandth part of our knowledge accumulated from life experiences. Put in organizational terms, we are individually quite poor at "transition planning." Our stores of knowledge go with us to the grave almost entirely whole, leaving each new generation to reinvent much knowledge that could have been its birthright.

It could be argued, of course, that most important knowledge achieved during individual human lives gets preserved in the form of books, journal and magazine articles, patents, documentaries, oral histories, and other means. By this logic, the loss of sheer quantity of human knowledge through mortality is adequately compensated for by preservation of quality of knowledge. In effect, we save the tip of the iceberg and therefore do not mourn the loss of the great unformed and unexamined mass of knowledge beneath the surface. For example, we cling to the works of Mozart (the tip of the iceberg) and are hardly aware of what it means to lose the capacity (i.e., the genius) to produce such works.

This is to say that true knowledge management must attend not merely to the totems of knowledge that survive individual mortality, but to the "database," the total knowledge-generalizing skills of a human being. Too often, we rush to harvest the fruits of knowledge while allowing the tree itself to wither, decay, and ultimately disappear. Knowledge management involves preserving as much of the "tree" as possible as well as the fruit it produces.

The death of knowledge for an organization occurs by means other than the mortality of its members. Firms that downsize without provision to preserve and extend necessary intellectual capital can find themselves brain dead after terminations and layoffs. After all, knowledge resides primarily within human heads; when "head count" is reduced, inevitably the sum of knowledge within the organization is reduced, sometimes critically so. This happens especially when a firm looks first to its highest paid, longest tenured employees as prime candidates for corporate bloodletting. From a financial management perspective, terminating a few high-paid employees may be less traumatic than firing many of the rank-and-file. But from a knowledge-management perspective, cutting off the experienced head from the working body may be foolish surgery indeed.

Knowledge can also die due to paradigm shifts. Aspects of knowledge that were important or sacred for one generation may cease to matter for another generation. Interpreting human character and health, for example, was inconceivable for Western medieval men and women apart from the theory of bodily "humors" (behavior-influencing fluids), such as phlegm, choler, and black bile. Their knowledge of these mysterious substances has become obsolete or anti-intellectual because the paradigms we use to understand mental and physical health have changed. Public schools now devote little time to the medieval humors ("Can Johnny recite the bodily symptoms attributable to black bile?") and most of us would object to their reintroduction. That knowledge has, by and large, vanished, and we see no reason for its resuscitation. Just as we have moved away from the medieval paradigm of humors, later generations may disdain our use of electroconvulsive therapy for depression, chemotherapy for cancer, or behavior-influencing drugs such as Prozac or Xanex.

When paradigm shifts occur, little intellectual effort is spent proving the past wrong. All knowledge resources quickly turn to the larger and apparently more promising task of proving the new vision right, or right-ish. No serious psychological study of the 20th century, for example, endeavors to compare the relative explanatory merits of the medieval theory of humors with the modern dispensation of Freudian, Jungian, or brain-chemistry theories. In short, when the paradigm shifts, the knowledge of the past is not "killed" or proven to be wrong. Instead, it is allowed to die from inattention. In this sense, paradigm shifts are largely rhetorical acts arising from the ability of new paradigm thinkers to provide powerful explanations of anomalies in the old paradigm.

Much is lost in such wholesale dismissal of the knowledge attached to old paradigms. Business organizations too easily find themselves embroiled in perpetual knowledge revolution ("Out with the old! In with the new!") rather than involved in meaningful knowledge growth. Knowledge management takes the death of knowledge seriously and accepts no paradigm shift on blind faith. Knowledge management seeks to understand causes for the failing health or death of knowledge. It memorializes and perpetuates what can and should be salvaged from the demise of a paradigm.

Finally, knowledge can die from too little or too much exercise. Unexercised knowledge, in the form of rote memorization of facts (the kings and queens of England, the capital cities of the states, the U.S. presidents in order, the books of the Bible, etc.), proves difficult for most of us. The task itself is not especially challenging (we easily memorize the names of dozens of friends and acquaintances), but most of us see it as useless. Knowledge unattached to purpose is short-lived. Those few among us who manage to become repositories of facts for their own sake are usually cast as social oddities—idiot savants of a sort—whose quick-recall ability is seen as little more than diverting and quaint. Winners of TV quiz shows such as *Jeopardy* hold great stores of knowledge but are unequipped to write great books, lead social movements, compose symphonies, or further scientific inquiry. Their knowledge is stillborn. It attaches itself to no larger purpose or design and *for that reason* falls into insignificance.

Knowledge management discourages the illusion that the amassing of facts, of and by itself, automatically leads to creative problem solving or meaningful innovation. The health of a knowledge base is measured not primarily by its physical size but by its agility and muscle tone. The ability to create and innovate adds far more value than the ability to recite historical trivia.

Curiously, knowledge can die as easily in an organization from too much exercise—that is, too rigid an agenda or predetermined purpose. If we are serious about finding cures for cancer, for example, our researchers must leave room in their methods and thinking for "happy accidents" or unexpected insights or test results that cast light down an entirely new avenue of investigation. Crucial discoveries, when they arrive, are almost always carried on the back of extraordinary labor. But the moment of their arrival, as in the case of Watson and Krick's discovery of the double-helix nature of DNA, often seems to be a gift, a moment of inspiration. Handel described such an experience after a furious 23 days composing *Messiah*. "My eyes," he tearfully told his wife, "were opened to the glory of God." Mathematicians and physicists from Newton to Einstein to Stephen Hawking have recorded similar experiences of sudden, quantum leaps in understanding and insight.

Knowledge management leaves room for and values the serendipitous. While still insisting upon them, it holds suspect the adequacy of its protocols and programs. It trusts that results will be forthcoming from established procedures while always hoping that lightning will strike, that a great idea or stunning insight will not flash upon the scene unseen or unappreciated.

Knowledge Can Be Owned

In spite of high literacy rates in developed countries, most knowledge valuable for increasing wealth is privately held. Knowledge unrelated to or marginally related to wealth is freely available because it serves no one's specific interest in the marketplace. Such free knowledge is the stuff of general education—history, literature, music, art, philosophy, cultural appreciation, languages, and so forth. In other words, the works of Shakespeare are available to all of us not because Shakespeare willed it so—he charged per view, in fact, as co-owner of the Globe Theatre—but because since Shakespeare's death no one has built an industry based on any kind of special or proprietary knowledge contained within his plays and poetry. The same cannot be said for the knowledge necessary to make paint, preserve food, make or repair computers, or remove air pollution. These and countless other technological and industrial functions are based on knowledge that is not made generally available. A company's "competitive advantage," in fact, often lies precisely in its privately held knowledge. Making paint may be easy, for all we in the general public know; but lacking the formula, we will continue to pay more for it per quart than we pay for wine.

Several implications fan out from the notion of privately owned knowledge. First, the identity of the owner must be clarified. Research and development personnel at computer, drug, cosmetic, and other similar companies routinely sign explicit and binding agreements with their employer that all knowledge accumulated, discovered, or developed during and after their employment remains the sole possession of the employer. No doubt Shakespeare had a similar understanding with actors in his troop, The King's Men, who individually may have been tempted to stage their own pirated versions of his plays (as in fact Shakespeare had pirated many from previous authors).

No matter how careful the wording of ownership agreements, of course, truly advantageous knowledge often has a way of "getting out," usually with devastating results in the marketplace. Netscape's "ownership" of Internet browsing technologies, for example, was closely imitated—some have said stolen—by Microsoft, with substantial market losses to Netscape. Knowledge management devises ways to determine what knowledge should be privately held and how it can be protected from competitors and clients.

Perhaps most successful of all in this regard is the way in which private knowledge was held by the Freemasons during and after the building of the great cathedrals in England and Europe beginning in the 11th century. The planning and skill necessary to build tall stone walls was closely guarded among masons, who rightly understood that their livelihood would suffer if less skilled and knowledgeable workmen were brought into their company. Secret passwords, handshakes, rings, and other symbols became identifying keys by which migrant masons could recognize fellows trained in their secrets of architecture, stonecutting, and building. Little was written down for fear of theft or copying. At secret meetings, leaders were sworn to loyalty and assigned to various "degrees" of authority within the brotherhood. So successful was this approach to knowledge management that long after the members had any secrets necessary to protect, the secret society continues with a life of its own, with hundreds of Masonic and similar guild-originated organizations still meeting in closed sessions, communicating by secret codes, dressing in unusual garb, and nurturing the tradition of a brotherhood with competitive advantage based on ownership of protected knowledge.

Modern organizations find unique ways to pierce the shield of privately held knowledge. In the many industries, companies acquire proprietary knowledge (friendly or hostile acquisitions, hiring away key employees, and reverse engineering products are common tactics). Then that knowledge is openly imitated, with the often-cynical strategy that legal challenges will take years in the courts to resolve—years during which the war for market share and profitability will be won and the issue of knowledge ownership will become moot.

By and large, companies have been unsuccessful in attempting to protect knowledge that drives sustained competitive advantage. Even products and processes that are patented or trademarked under the laws of one country are stolen by companies not vulnerable to legal or political sanctions from that country. The blatant theft of U.S. television technology in the 1960s by Asian competitors is a classic example. So devastating was this loss of proprietary knowledge that, for all intents and purposes, the U.S. television manufacturing industry ceased to exist by 1980. Similar "borrowing" has occurred more recently in the chip making, disk drives, and telecommunications device industries. U.S. manufacturers have largely given up efforts to stop knowledge piracy through international courts or through the American political system. Instead, U.S. manufacturers have adopted a "first/best/least" philosophy of hitting the marketplace first and hard with new products, maintaining quality standards, and pricing products at levels that discourage start-up enterprises from copying them.

At best, however, this appears to be a desperation strategy that conceives and develops new markets only to give them over eventually to the idea pirates. The impetus falls upon American companies to continually innovate—and convince the marketplace to purchase "new"—while foreign competitors play a waiting game based on serving mass markets with inexpensive imitations.

Effective knowledge management assesses what knowledge must be protected for competitive advantage, how that knowledge will be protected, and to what degree legal and political entities can be trusted to enforce laws related to ownership of intellectual properties.

Knowledge Is Immanent as Well as Extant

Not all knowledge worth managing in an organization is explicit and visible. Much organizational knowledge is held in creative reserve in the form of human resources and computer expert systems. This immanent and preformed knowledge has the potential for becoming extant and formed at any moment, just as the energy within a battery can be tapped when needed.

A brain surgeon's expertise and capacity for action is an example of immanent knowledge. After years of study and practice, few brain surgeons can list the items within their knowledge bases. Surgeons' core competencies lie in immanent knowledge—deep wells of insight, reflection, memory, and intuition that can be summoned when the need arises. The visible, extant "spark" of correct decisions and actions come to the fore in life-and-death circumstances. Similar knowledge banks are in the minds of virtually all personnel who exercise creative, thinking functions within organizations. Artificial intelligence is often aimed at this kind of knowledge and one theorist has predicted that computer IQ will exceed human IQ by the midpoint of this century.

Immanent knowledge remains a challenging but crucially important aspect of knowledge management. Just as brain surgeons must create and maintain their immanent knowledge, organizations may use knowledge management to preserve such vital knowledge. This prospect forces us to confront several key questions. How does one nurture immanent knowledge without force-feeding it in a disruptive way? Further, how does one monitor immanent knowledge to ensure that its store of resources is increasingly vital and relevant to the needs of the organization? Finally, how does an organization prevent unnecessary redundancy in immanent knowledge? How many people need specialized procedures that only a few will ever perform? Hasty answers are dangerous because the absence of such knowledge inhibits "spin-off" insights and may corrupt decision making in related areas. In short, a degree of redundancy in immanent knowledge resources probably is desirable if it encourages wholeness of vision and broad perspective in decision making.

Knowledge Can Be Stored

It can safely be estimated that more knowledge has been externalized (that is, made observable and preservable) in the last 20 years than in the entire previous history of mankind. On paper, film, tape, and above all by electronic storage means we have "lent our minds out," in Milton's phrase. For example, 12,000 new sites *per week* continue to appear on the Internet.

But now that we have so energetically externalized knowledge we face an unexpected and ironic problem: how to internalize knowledge again. Getting knowledge out of our heads and onto disks or paper was a feat of technology; getting facts back into our heads for practical and creative use is a task that involves much more than technology.

The central intellectual work of the 21st century may lie not so much in accumulating externalized banks of knowledge as in developing time-efficient ways to process selected portions of that knowledge through a chip whose essential circuits have not and will not change: the chip between the ears. "Real-time" internalization of knowledge may be the most imposing challenge. A training videotape or movie, for example, cannot be internalized by the human mind using a "fast-forward" technique. The tape must be played in real time for human learning to take place. Traditional lectures and much educational software are similarly bound by real-time constraints. By contrast, still photos and, to a lesser degree, book or magazine pages can be accessed in "mind time," with the roving intellectual eye free to locate and select bits of content without also involving the entire surrounding context. CD, videodisk, and "computer search" technologies offer similar accessibility without the necessity to play through a cohesive context to ferret out a desired bit of content.

Lacking such accessibility, vast stores of knowledge may fall into chaotic and useless heaps. Critics of the Internet argue that its enormous potential, as a truly global externalization of millions of minds, will prove vacuous unless we can solve the problem of accessibility. Whereas the human mind sorts and prioritizes ideas and images, the Internet merely gathers and collects. Even the more sophisticated search engines available do not facilitate similar prioritization.

The most poignant example of this dilemma lies in the efforts of elementary schools to "get wired" to the Internet and thereby enhance the accessible knowledge and experience base of their students. But when well-intentioned teachers advise students to search for information on topics of interest, both teachers and students quickly confront the chaos of knowledge that currently characterizes the Internet. A second-grader searching for information on "goldfish" using the Infoseek search engine was dumbfounded and discouraged to confront more than 100,000 "hits" for his search term—with the option, adding insult to injury, to seeing them 10 at a time. ("Click to see the next ten.") Where does one begin to make sense or use out of a knowledge base that lacks familiar search paths, or heuristics, congenial to human learning and reflection? In the case of the second-grader, what meta-level of knowledge specification could have and should have been provided to make the micro-level of millions of factoids quickly searchable and therefore useful?

The immediate challenge facing the Internet is to prevent cancerous growth—that is, wildly accretive expansion without regard for internal organization, connective tissue, or, for that matter, the health of the surrounding organism. Paradoxically, we can access the Internet faster than ever before only to find, once we get there, that the Net is slower than ever in divulging the knowledge we desire. Knowledge management is impossible apart from a system of organization that makes knowledge accessible and useful.

KNOWLEDGE CAN BE CATEGORIZED

In addition to the distinctions already suggested between immanent and extant knowledge, the various types of knowledge common within an organization can be enumerated.

Label knowledge is the vast catalog of names that we attach to the flora and fauna that make up the jungle of our particular organization. As a practical organizational necessity, names for things matter for day-to-day operations and efficiency. But label knowledge too often becomes an obsessive-compulsive totem for minds that equate organizational learning with mastery of jargon and labels. In such an environment, newcomers to the organization are pilloried by old-timers until the ingenues are able to speak the specialized language of terms, tags, and titles correctly. Entire cultures within branches of the military, academic disciplines, and the professions are built up in large part of such sensitivity to label knowledge. God help the "grunt" who doesn't know the internal label language of the Army—or the sociologist, for that matter, who accidentally calls a spade a spade. It goes almost without saying that label knowledge makes up an exclusionary wall by which lawyers separate themselves, expensively, from the world of common sense and forthright expression.

Process knowledge involves knowing how things work, even if one cannot name all components active within the process (i.e., label knowledge). Business environments value process knowledge on the micro-level—engineers who know how a heating system operates, for example—but often fail to recognize the importance of process knowledge at the macro-level. This has occurred, and still occurs, in spite of nearly a decade of Business Process Reengineering that explicitly focused management attention on gaining knowledge about processes. How can one describe the core processes at work in a large organization such as General Electric or Bank of America? Individually, each employee knows (or should know) the processes in which he or she is involved. But what can be said of larger process patterns—and who is in a position to observe and describe those processes?

Knowledge management should pay attention to both the micro- and macro-levels of process knowledge. If the macro-level process is the building of a pyramid, for example, that knowledge influences the specific work of stonecutters and laborers at the micro-level. But, beyond a vague notion of increasing shareholder value, too many organizations despair of attaining process knowledge at such a macro-level. In effect, they do not know whether they are building a pyramid or a coliseum, but their employees had better be quick about doing so.

Skill knowledge is knowing how to do something of value to the organization. This level of knowledge has long been managed devotedly by companies through job descriptions, training programs, performance evaluations, and other means. But once skill sets have been determined, companies tend to look upon them as unchanging constellations in the night sky—patterns that are "there" along with the furniture at the company. These skill sets become the basis of most hiring, and hence define the overall core competencies of the organization.

The coming era requires a much more fluid view of skill knowledge. Computer companies have already found that an employee's ability to *learn* quickly and well is an infinitely more valuable skill in a rapidly changing business environment than is a more vocationally oriented, specific skill. Knowledge management for the new century requires that skill knowledge be defined and developed so that new patterns (constellations of skill points) can come together quickly to meet emerging market needs.

People knowledge. This diffuse but vitally important category of knowledge comprises all the insights, intuitions, and relational information we use to work with other people. In the iceberg analogy previously cited, this kind of knowledge is truly subsurface but vast within organizations. Usually it is managed ineffectively or not at all precisely because of its lack of visibility. Few companies think about what knowledge their employees should have about one another's motives, communication styles, or professional goals. Interestingly, the same companies expect employees to congeal into efficient, cohesive work teams but devote little thought to the people knowledge that makes such teams possible.

Knowledge management brings people knowledge to visibility and to a position of prominence in a framework for understanding and using knowledge within the corporation.

CONCLUSION

There are numerous definitions of knowledge management, one of the primary foci of this book. An article on the subject in *Information Week* produced the following definition:

A way or concept of doing business that revolves around the following four processes:

- Gathering: Bringing information and data into the system.
- Organizing: Associating items to subjects, establishing context, making them easier to find.
- Refining: Adding value by discovering relationships, abstracting, synthesizing, and sharing.
- Disseminating: Getting knowledge to the people who can use it.[1]

There is no currently accepted single definition of knowledge. And, there is no widespread agreement on the overall parameters of knowledge. However, we will attempt to flesh out this powerful new management movement through:

- Theoretical perspectives that help frame discussion of the subject.
- A review of its impact on general economic thinking.
- Examples of knowledge management practices.
- A review of ways to measure the impact of knowledge assets.
- A framework for reviewing the electronic tools for managing knowledge.
- A series of implementation heuristics to help managers get started.
- A discussion of the future for this new management movement.

The following chapters will investigate the components and implications of knowledge management. It is important to recognize, however, that the field of knowledge management (unlike, let's say, biology or physics) has not yet been systematized to the point that it can accurately be called a "science." Much remains speculative in this infancy stage of knowledge management—and with that stage comes inevitable frustration to those who seek uncontroverted answers. But there is at the same time the joy of discovery and the exhilaration of exploration in these early years of a new, powerful

---

[1]Jeff Angus and Jeetu Patel, "Knowledge Management: Great Concept but What Is It?" *Information Week,* March 16, 1998.

field of inquiry. The authors welcome readers as participants in the forming of a new science. We hope to stimulate critical thinking and creative new approaches to managing and measuring knowledge as well as providing managers useful tools for increasing the value added by their organizations' knowledge assets.

QUESTIONS FOR REVIEW

1. What are the basic parameters for knowledge management?
2. How can these be used to guide development of a framework for knowledge management programs in organizations?
3. What is your personal definition of knowledge? How does this definition guide your approach to managing knowledge?
4. What knowledge management parameters are missing from the discussion?
5. What are the practical limitations of trying to define knowledge?
6. How do these limitations make our approaches to managing knowledge problematic?

CASE STUDY: Big Brands Foods, Inc.

A Knowledge Management Case

Since their inception and popular acceptance at midcentury, coupons have been the bane of the retail food industry. Even though expensive to distribute and redeem, these pesky bits of paper had seemed a necessary evil in the ongoing war for market share among major food stores.

Until the Bonus Card. Beginning in early 1998, Big Brands Food Stores, Inc., led an industry revolution by doing away with coupons. The Bonus Card is a plastic card that credits purchasers with discounts on an ever-changing variety of food, health, and home supply products. Using the Bonus Card is simple compared to the old days of collecting and sorting coupons. Customers simply show the Bonus Card at the checkout stand and their savings are automatically credited to their purchase amount. Because the number on the card is the person's telephone number, most checkers dispense with seeing the plastic card and just ask for the customer's number.

The Bonus Card approach to attracting and holding customers is a resounding success. The company saves in excess of 40 percent of the expenses involved in coupon publication and redemption.

The Bonus Card program began innocently enough as an expedient alternative to coupons. Big Brands Food Stores, however, soon realized that the program was generating a gold mine of data on customer preferences and purchasing patterns. Day by day, the company's mainframe computer accumulates an exact inventory of purchases—by item, price, and time of day—for each customer participating in the Bonus Card program, and well over 80 percent of store customers held Bonus Cards by October 1998. These customers were known to the computer not just by telephone number but, by easy interface with telephone company records, by name and street address. The computer could specify, for example, that Mr. C. J. Jones of 187 Ocean Ave., San Francisco, spent $214 on over-the-counter pharmaceutical and health-related purchases in the past six months, and could further list the specific items purchased (a heavy reliance on sleep-inducing medications, it turns out).

Deciding what to do with this mushrooming database of otherwise private information was the next step. The company first began to extract meaningful information from its data heap by seeking generalized customer profiles for the purpose of more targeted marketing. For example, the company discovered one profile (22 percent of its customers) purchased food items but no health-related or cleaning products. The company seized the opportunity of broadening its range of sales to these customers by mailing them advertising booklets featuring specific discounts on health-related and cleaning products. Another customer profile (after 8:00 P.M. shoppers) showed a preponderance of prepared-food, deli, and snack-food purchasers. This information influenced the way the store stocked and displayed such items and the hours it allotted for deli personnel.

While the program is an outstanding success, potential problems began to develop. Insurance companies, brand vendors, HMOs, and even the IRS requested access to the information gold mine. Insurance companies would use the data to rate the insurability of new applicants. Brand vendors wanted to know who was buying their product, when, where, and for how much. HMOs felt that customers with a record of high expenses for pharmaceuticals would be ideal targets for HMO advertising. And the IRS wanted to use individual gross expenditures at the food store as a means of detecting unreported income.

Because profit margins at the stores seldom exceed 2 percent, management was engaged by the prospect of selling information to interested third parties. However, before acting on such requests, the company has decided to convene a closed-door meeting of top company executives and information systems specialists.

The questions before them are important ones: What policies should guide knowledge management in the company? What uses should be made of the company's growing base of specific customer information? What should customers be told about how this information will be used by the company or others? Should customer consent be obtained for the use of existing information or the gathering of future information? Who should be allowed access to such information? Can access be denied to the IRS, FBI, federal and state regulators, and others? Should the Bonus Card program be continued? Expanded? These questions lie at the heart of knowledge management.

2

THE KNOWLEDGE–
BASED ECONOMY

A sense of history with regard to the "knowledge economy" and just what is meant by this term provide a backdrop against which the claims for the knowledge economy can be calibrated. Let's make sure we know what we mean by a "knowledge economy." Every economy has relied on knowledge as its base—an agrarian economy, for example, relies on thorough knowledge of planting, harvesting, and so forth. If by "knowledge economy" we mean that knowledge per se is for sale, then the Greeks, Romans, and medieval church were prime examples of economies where ideas including philosophies and theologies were the main output or "product" of major economic institutions including the Church. In our era, universities are primary examples of places where knowledge is for sale.

Although knowledge has made significant contributions to other economic structures, the current economy is unique in one respect. Investors assign value to businesses based on estimates of the future value of a business's present knowledge and knowledge-generating capacity. This phenomenon began with the Industrial Revolution and continued with the emergence of stock speculators. In contrast, earlier approaches placed greater value on the ownership of tangible assets. For example, in an agrarian society, the value of a farm was based on land, equipment, and seeds, not on the farmer's ability to apply his knowledge of farming.

It would be interesting to list businesses that make a profit on access to, and distribution of knowledge per se. These businesses would include Internet search engines, newspapers, television, radio, the church in all its forms, universities and schools of all kinds, and any company willing to sell its knowledge. For each of these institutions, knowledge *is* the product. Added together, purveyors of knowledge itself comprise a growing percentage of the American economic machine, as well as the global economy.

PRODUCTS AND SERVICES

Managing knowledge in a knowledge economy, therefore, means looking at more than purveyors of knowledge per se. The first step in creating a theory of knowledge management applicable to our economy is to discard the idea that most organizations are exemplars of the knowledge economy. All organizations—businesses and others alike—use knowledge to create, build, and distribute products and/or services.

Knowledge management has to be designed to apply to businesses that use their knowledge to build products/services that customers are willing to buy. The majority of knowledge management applications in our economy have to do with how to acquire and embed knowledge in the core processes that ultimately create competitive advantage.[1]

With these reservations in mind, this chapter focuses on the characteristics of the knowledge economy and the ways executives can leverage their use of knowledge assets to create value and competitive advantage. Most corporate leaders are understandably better versed in management techniques focused on operational efficiency, skill development, product and service distribution, and the like. These men and women find the new economic order both threatening and enticing: threatening because skills they have honed no longer guarantee success; enticing because new challenges and opportunities await.

Executives have focused more often than not on people and resources as tangible assets that could be moved, replaced, or eliminated as business needs dictated. For example, business process reengineering typically resulted in downsizing. Managers of this ilk have difficulty conceiving the corporation as a set of knowledge assets that are deployed through people, processes, and technology. This lack of insight may spell disaster in the increasingly fast-paced electronic economy where the highest leverage is derived from intangible assets such as knowledge.

In the electronic economy, market successes can be undercut overnight by a competitor's knowledge edge—a competitive advantage that leads directly to the preferred product or service in the marketplace. Market leadership, size, name recognition, and structure are no longer guarantees of survival. Being in the *right* place and time with the *right knowledge* matters most. And "right" presumes the shrewd acquisition, application, and management of knowledge that fits the needs of the marketplace in a given time and place. In the knowledge-based economy, the companies with the right answers to the felt needs of their stakeholders and clientele will earn and deserve their success.

CHALLENGES AND OPPORTUNITIES

Industry now faces a dramatically new competitive environment replete with dynamic opportunities, possibilities, and challenges. With industry evolving at an ever-increasing rate, companies in the electronic economy are faced with the need to create strong positions using tools that will transform them in order to capitalize on these explosive new growth opportunities. However, a number of significant challenges and unprecedented pressures must be resolved to successfully thrive in this new competitive environment.

---

[1]R. Chase and T. Housel, "Service Theory and Knowledge Value-Added," in press; Thomas J. Housel and Valery Kanevsky, "Reengineering Business Processes: A Complexity Theory Approach to Value Added," *INFOR*, 33 (1995), pp. 248–62; Thomas J. Housel and Sandra Hom, *Knowledge Management in the Telecommunications Industry.* Refereed research report: International Engineering Consortium and Center for Telecommunication Management, 1999.

One challenge is particularly pressing: The electronic marketplace is changing rapidly and executives need to ensure that their employees and systems have access to the knowledge that is critical for supporting and sustaining their visions for success. Another equally daunting task is that of capturing new customers and markets while simultaneously retaining existing ones. Success in providing new access to critical knowledge, while simultaneously capturing new customers and retaining existing ones, lies in identifying and deploying "knowledge assets." They must systemize and display knowledge that leads to enhanced services, products, and features in order to sustain and create value. Thriving in the new competitive market requires companies to make effective investments in knowledge tools that contribute to strategic direction while overcoming knowledge gaps.

A few companies are now experimenting with knowledge management initiatives to capture and capitalize on knowledge assets. Nortel, IBM, and Cisco[2] are among the leaders. They are using knowledge management to improve profitability, transform themselves, and capture current employee knowledge and train new hires. While these leaders have helped to launch the revolution, success in the new economy requires companies to make their knowledge management initiatives ubiquitous. Determining how to do this is the key to success in the knowledge economy.

ECONOMY IN TRANSITION

Global markets are expanding rapidly. Double-digit growth in information and knowledge management technology equipment and services is expected to continue through the year 2001.[3] For example, the global market for communications services currently generates revenues of approximately $725 billion, and global telecommunications revenues are estimated to climb 400 percent to $3 trillion by 2003. More importantly:

- Economies are becoming more knowledge based, and consumers everywhere demand more, better, and faster access to information.
- There are currently over 250 million global wireless customers, with one billion expected by 2003.
- Future growth will be driven by data transmission, with these revenues doubling over the next three years—a growth rate 5 times that of voice transmissions.[4]

Information services and the companies that provide them are dramatically transforming the way people and businesses communicate, live, work, and play. The industry is facing a number of challenges and opportunities. New technologies threaten to make today's systems and networks obsolete; nimble, bright, and aggressive new competitors threaten to upset existing markets and infrastructures; and today's consumers, who have been encouraged to regard the new as the best are eternally on the verge of bolting for the latest and greatest, upsetting years of nurturing by providers of equipment and

---

[2]Knowledge Management in Telecom's Industry Conference Brochure, 1997.
[3]Smith speech, February 26, 1998.
[4]Seidenberg, April 24, 1998.

services. Nowhere can the past, present, and future of the struggle between these opposing forces be seen more clearly than in the information-technology-driven marketplace.

Brave New World

By global standards, U.S. information companies and services are the most innovative, most productive, and most competitively priced in the world. However, they now face the challenges that many dominant companies such as Chase Manhattan and American Express have in the past. These companies were forced to globalize their businesses and practices to meet aggressive foreign competition as they entered new markets. Today, companies must reinvent themselves by modernizing their information infrastructures, reducing costs, increasing the value they provide customers, diversifying knowledge assets, and merging businesses in order to respond effectively to the new market realities.

These new market realities revolve around the explosive growth of information in its many varied forms. With this new reality comes new opportunities, requirements, and responsibilities. There are new rules to follow and to be made, new competitors to defend against, and new customer expectations to meet. Traditional companies must update legacy systems and information infrastructures quickly. Many are tethered to large legacy systems that were not designed to support Information Age products and services. In addition, most plant and equipment was designed to handle industrial-era products and services. Further complicating matters, changes in these areas must be made while companies simultaneously struggle to enter new markets and compete with new entrants in their core markets.

Many traditional industries have been experiencing a frenzy of restructuring, acquisitions, and dealmaking. Even though most of these companies were born in the Industrial Age, they must move beyond the traditional benefits of merging functional areas, that is, cost efficiencies from consolidations. They must seek new leverage from merging knowledge assets by finding better ways of deploying those assets in core processes. The problem for investors and corporate executives is finding the benefits of merging knowledge assets:

- What knowledge assets have we acquired?
- What is the value of these assets?
- Which company's core knowledge assets are providing the best returns?
- How should the joint knowledge assets be deployed in core processes to produce the highest returns?

Table 2.1 lists a number of very large mergers and acquisitions.

The Global Brave New World

This drive to consolidate industries is the result of dynamic global forces. The trend is nowhere more evident than in the global telecommunications industry. The forces driving this move in the telecommunications industry include:

TABLE 2.1   LARGE MERGERS IN THE UNITED STATES

Rank	Companies	Date Announced	Value (Billions)
1	Travelers Group/Citicorp*	April 6, 1998	$70.0
2	NationsBank/BankAmerica*	April 13, 1998	$59.0
3	SBC Communications/Ameritech*	May 11, 1998	$56.0
4	Daimler-Benz/Chrysler*	May 7, 1998	$38.6
5	WorldCom/MCI Communications*	October 1, 1997	$35.3
6	Banc One/First Chicago NBD	April 13, 1998	$28.9
7	Kohlberg Kravis Roberts/RJR Nabisco	October 24, 1988	$24.6
8	Bank of New York/Mellon Bank*	April 22, 1998	$23.3
9	Bell Atlantic/Nynex	April 22, 1996	$19.5
10	First Union/CoreStates Financial	November 18, 1997	$19.5

*Announced but not completed.
Source: Karen Kaplan, "When SBC Comes Calling," *Los Angeles Times,* May 12, 1998.

- *Explosion of New Technologies:* Advances in digital, wireless, and optical technologies are creating incredible new communications capacity. Applications are being developed that use these advances to establish global, one-number, go-anywhere, high-speed, multi-megabit, wired or wireless, do-everything communications.
- *Phenomenal Increase in Demand for Data Communications:* This demand has outpaced all projections and is growing at five times the speed of voice traffic. Data will soon surpass, if it hasn't already, voice traffic on global networks.
- *Synchronous Advent of the Internet, Intranets, and Extranets as Strategic Tools:* Some experts say Internet Protocol, or IP-based packet[5] networks, may soon render traditional circuit-switched networks obsolete. These types of networks are the networks of choice for the boom in data traffic. PCs now outsell TVs, and e-mail delivers five times more information than the post office, while the number of Internet users doubled in the past year to 50 million.
- *Arrival of Sophisticated Internet Telephony:* Although it is still an imperfect technology, it will tap a potential multibillion market within five years.
- *Global Deregulation:* This moves hand-in-hand with the forces noted above, and is driven by national governments, international organizations, and market forces. It is strengthened by a palpable demand the world over to be part of the global community and integrated into the world economy.

Around the world, the historic expansion of communications markets is racing ahead. Governments are seeking to ignite a cycle of growth, innovation, and investment through sweeping deregulatory agreements. By the end of 1998, 80 percent of the world's telecom markets were scheduled to be liberalized. In addition, the directives of

[5]Fife et al., Presentation on Internet Protocol Telephony to the National Communications Forum, October 1999, Chicago, Illinois.

the European Union and the World Trade Organization (WTO) will cover more than 90 percent of global markets when fully ratified.

These patterns ensure continued movement toward a comprehensive information technology infrastructure to support new and improved ways to distribute and deploy knowledge assets, increase the impact and importance of systems, technology, strategy, and knowledge over central planning, and reduce government influence over business. The global economy affects all industries. The survival of individual firms linked directly to the intense global competition is often precarious at best. Firms that are capable of combining systems, technology, and networks to enable better knowledge management will lead the way in setting standards, establishing industry benchmarks, and meeting the challenges of the future, and they will be the ones that survive.

In an ever-changing world, knowledge will play an increasingly vital role in establishing competitive and strategic advantage. The role of knowledge assets is one of the prime determinants of success in the future.

KNOWLEDGE-BASED ECONOMIES

The global economy has decisively entered a new age. It is variously called the "Information Age," the "Third Wave," or the "Electronic Economy." Regardless of the terminology, these names and others refer to the transition that has taken place in the economies of the industrialized nations, followed closely by the developing nations. Although there are a few economies primarily involved in supporting traditional manufacturing industries, the future of development and growth is clearly centered on automated manufacturing and information-dependent service industries. It is estimated that more than 50 percent of gross domestic product (GDP) in the major Organization for Economic Co-Operation and Development (OECD) countries is now knowledge-based and heavily reliant on information technology. These economies can be called knowledge-based economies.[6] Knowledge-based economies are those that are directly based on the production, distribution, and use of knowledge and information in the design, production, and distribution of products and especially services.

While knowledge, embedded in systems, brains, and technology, has always been the key to economic development, in recent years its importance has been steadily increasing. The OECD economies are more strongly dependent on the production, distribution, and use of knowledge than ever before. Output and employment are expanding fastest in high-technology industries, such as computers, electronics, communications, and aerospace. During the past decade, the high-technology share of OECD manufacturing production and exports has more than doubled, to reach 20–25 percent.

In addition, high-technology industries, particularly leading-edge electronics and information technology industries, are driving economic growth around the world. According to industry estimates, the markets for computer and communications hardware and services and for software have grown to over $1 trillion.

[6]OECD report on the Knowledge-Based Economy, 1996.

Impact of the Knowledge Economy

One characteristic of the knowledge-based economy is the high demand for skilled technical workers. Nowhere is this characteristic more pronounced than in the United States. Already almost 60 percent of all American workers are knowledge workers of some sort, and 8 of 10 new jobs are in information-intensive sectors of the economy. The service sector, now representing 70 percent of U.S. GDP, is increasingly information technology intensive.[7] The U.S. government is constantly under pressure to relax immigration policies to allow companies to bring in increased numbers of high-tech employees to meet the supply shortfall in the domestic market.

According to the Information Technology Association of America (ITAA) there are approximately 190,000 specialized information technology jobs in the United States that are unfilled. The U.S. Department of Labor predicts that new and expanding technologies will account for 80 percent of new jobs in the next 10 years, and the Bureau of Labor Statistics projected that the United States would require more than one million new IT workers (computer scientists and engineers, systems analysts, and computer programmers) between 1994 and 2005—on average, 95,000 new jobs to fill each year.

It was predicted that by the year 2000, over 60 percent of new jobs would require computer skills (50 percent require them today) and almost 65 percent would be jobs performed by "knowledge workers"—people whose livelihoods revolve around the information they generate and receive.[8]

Knowledge Capital

Accelerating the conversion of knowledge into financial gains using Information Age alchemy is the real challenge for contemporary companies.

The key to generating economic growth and value in industrial-based economies was the accumulation of fixed, tangible assets, measured as capital investment. The knowledge economy is one where intangible assets or knowledge, in its various forms, combine with information technology and network infrastructure to drive growth and value creation. Knowledge assets include information and knowledge stored in patents, copyrights, corporate data warehouses, employees' brains, processes (e.g., work rules), and information systems. These tools and systems have been used to leverage employee knowledge in pursuit of improvements to core processes. Just as the means of production in the Industrial Age was industrial capital (plant, equipment, machinery), in today's economy the means of production is knowledge capital.

The information technology industry plays a central role in these activities. The tools to store, disseminate, and manage these vital corporate assets are provided by companies in this industry. Specifically, the network companies provide the platform for moving knowledge, information, and raw data to diverse locations where it is used

[7]Don Tapscott, *The Digital Economy*, 1995.
[8]America's New Deficit: The Shortage of Information Technology Workers, press release, September 29, 1997; Thomas A. Stewart, *Intellectual Capital: The New Wealth of Organizations*, 1997.

to complete essential core processes, and to the end-users who pay for services and products within which knowledge assets are embedded.

Likewise, the information systems companies provide the tools to manage these knowledge assets as they are used to produce products and services. These two industries have been in the process of merging (explicitly by acquisition or implicitly by assuming the functions of the other) for at least the last two decades.

Witness the fact that IBM is now providing networking services for its primary corporate customers, and WorldCom/MCI and AT&T are providing Internet and systems support and integration services for their residential and business customers. IBM has developed a wave division multiplexing scheme for fiber-optic transmission that allows 40 gigabites per channel. Scott G. McNealy, CEO of Sun Microsystems Inc., and Larry Ellison, CEO of Oracle, have been advocating "network-centric" computing.

Accelerating this merging of functions are these new business realities:

- Globalization
- Intense rivalry and "hyper-competition"
- Technological change
- Customer expectations
- Deregulation
- New competitors
- New technologies
- Industry consolidation[9]

Among these new business realities, two stand out as having particularly dramatic impacts on the evolving nature of the knowledge economy: globalization and hyper-competition.

Global deregulation allows new competitors to enter previously protected national monopolies. Personal communication services (PCS) and wireless services are offering serious competition to landline local exchange carriers and long-distance carriers. Call-back services offer competition to national carriers throughout much of the globe, seriously undercutting revenues. Microsoft's Bill Gates is engaged in a satellite communication venture, "Teledesic," that will provide interactive (potentially broadband) services. Other globe-encircling satellite systems are offering, for the first time in many places, real alternatives to national telephone (landline) monopolies, and are creating huge upheavals in these markets. AT&T's acquisition of NCR (even though it has since sold the company) was part of its broad strategy to offer its customers both network and information systems products and services as it recreates itself with a significant Internet focus.

Hyper-competition is forcing information technology companies to offer services and products that provide complete, one-stop solutions to meet customers' increasingly demanding expectations. Executives expect integrated systems solutions, not just the isolated pieces of information systems and network services. And if these are not avail-

---

[9]Thomas Housel and Eric Skopec, *Global Telecommunication Revolution: The Business Perspective,* (New York: McGraw-Hill Companies), 2001.

able from current suppliers, there are competitors who will provide them. Companies such as IBM and Electronic Data Systems are providing complete services to their large international clients and complete solutions for their large business customers by integrating information system and network services.

In the consumer market, companies are now racing to build the systems and products that will meet the market demand for integrated services. The future clearly will be a place of continuous consolidation and fractious rivalry among industries as market demand and technological evolution drive them into each other's territories. And the key to meeting this demand and evolutionary imperative is, and will continue to be, knowledge.

Value vs. Cost of Knowledge Assets

Knowledge assets are different from the capital and labor assets of the Industrial Age. Unlike traditional assets and inventory, knowledge is neither finite nor scarce. It is used without being consumed. A critical difference is that the cost of acquiring knowledge is not directly related to its value in the market.

For example, Merck & Co. and Eli Lilly made approximately the same investments in R & D from 1980 to 1988. However, the market value of the output of those investments, measured by the market value of the outputs themselves, was much higher for Merck than for Eli Lilly.[10] While not conclusive, this suggests that investments in corporate knowledge must be strategically driven, fostered, and nurtured in a comprehensive way to ensure that they create value measurable in the form of cash flows from new products/services and cost savings to operations. The value of the output, rather than the cost of the asset acquisition, represents the true value of knowledge assets to a company.

Intangible vs. Tangible Assets

Traditional balance sheets listing tangible assets and liabilities no longer adequately portray the current or future value of knowledge-intensive companies. Balance sheets are useful in determining the value of companies when this value consists of tangible assets and traditional capital investment. When the assets are intangible, the value of companies is problematic to define using traditional methodologies. Since much of the value of knowledge-based companies is intangible, balance sheets cannot accurately represent the true market value of these companies.[11]

The Knowledge Organization in the New Economy

For companies competing in the knowledge economy, the ability to identify and leverage knowledge assets plays a critical role. Failure to do so can lead to dramatically negative consequences, including the failure to realize markets, revenues, and growth

---

[10]John Rutledge, "You're a Fool If You Buy This Stuff," *Forbes ASAP,* April 3, 1997.
[11]Thomas Stewart, *Intellectual Capital,* 1997.

opportunities. For example, Xerox has long been at the forefront of new knowledge generation through its Palo Alto Research Center (PARC). PARC spawned, among others, the computer industry's most popular networking standard, Ethernet, and the icon-based graphical desktop metaphor that later became the Apple user interface and ultimately the metaphor for all desktop computing.[12] However, Xerox did not capitalize on the majority of those innovations and has lost billions in revenue.

In 1996 Xerox formed Xerox New Enterprises (XNE), a holding company intended to commercialize ideas generated from Xerox's Palo Alto Research Center (PARC). XNE is Xerox's attempt to create a new paradigm to take advantage of innovations and technologies that fall outside of the company's core competencies and main markets.

Microsoft, according to knowledge strategist Paul Strassmann, is one of the supreme masters at leveraging its knowledge assets. Strassmann calculates Microsoft's knowledge capital as being between $67 billion and $91.6 billion.[13] Using a methodology that he calls Knowledge Capital, Strassmann estimated the value of Microsoft's intangible resources by taking the company's stock market valuation of $98.6 billion at the end of 1996 and subtracting its $7 billion in financial assets.[14]

Another company Strassmann cites as being extremely adept at generating Knowledge Capital is Coca-Cola. According to Strassmann, "[T]hey sell water with a little sugar and bubbles. It is their intimate knowledge of the marketplace, their brand name advertising and relationships with their distribution outlets that create their superior valuation."[15]

Accounting for the market value of companies in the knowledge economy requires an understanding of how they create future cash flows from their operations. Since these operations are largely knowledge intensive, effectively managing knowledge assets is the best predictor of these future positive cash flows. However, this requires a reconceptualization of the company as a group of knowledge assets that are deployed in a variety of forms to meet varying needs. These assets include people, information technology, policies, work rules, and processes. Each must be managed effectively to create positive cash flows. With knowledge as the predictor of value, a new approach to understanding the corporation becomes possible.

Capitalizing on knowledge assets can mean the difference between survival and extinction in today's economy. Because they rely so heavily on knowledge assets, information intensive companies are particularly vulnerable to the failure to utilize these assets strategically.

The Internet   One of the defining requirements of competing in the knowledge economy is that heavy investment is required to be "in the game," but there are no explicit or implicit guarantees of future revenue flows. Nowhere is this phenomena more apparent than in the Internet industry.

---

[12]Thomas Koulopoulos, *Corporate Instinct: Building a Knowing Enterprise for the 21st Century,* 1997.
[13]P. A. Strassmann, "The Business Value of Computers."
[14]"Taking the Measure of Knowledge Assets," *Computerworld,* April 6, 1998.
[15]"Leading Lights: Knowledge Strategist Paul Strassmann," Knowledge Executive Report, October 1996.

Some industry experts think that within a decade the Internet will become ubiquitous in the United States, and developed nations will reach this plateau within 15 years. This growth will result in a global market where only 50 percent of Internet users live in the United States. Moreover, Internet traffic now accounts for about 50 percent of all data transmissions, and this traffic is doubling every four months.[16]

Writer Kevin Kelly notes that one of the catalysts for the explosion of the Internet was the collapse in network charges during the late 1980s when suddenly it was feasible to send data almost anywhere at anytime at reasonable rates. Suddenly it made more sense to e-mail and transmit data than to mail, messenger, or express documents. MCI president Timothy Price notes, "In the last decade, telecommunications—moving information and moving capital at the rate of one trillion dollars a day—has become one of the most important, [and] some say, the most important, element of our national business infrastructure."[17]

Managing Knowledge in the New Economy   The competitive environment is now characterized by new technologies, increasingly sophisticated customers, and eager new competitors. The market opportunity for companies requires giving customers more innovative products and value.

To capitalize on these trends, the companies are facing the need for significant investments in and management of all their knowledge assets: employees, networks, and information systems. To do this, corporations must be able to track the ongoing effect of their investments on the cash flows they generate. Such tracking has rarely been practiced, primarily because most lack effective methodologies to evaluate the value of intangible knowledge assets. However, given the rapid pace of consolidation in the industry, efficient and effective initiatives designed to capture and utilize knowledge are critical to realize the benefits of consolidation.

In the past, the lack of these measurement tools has resulted in unintended depletion of knowledge assets. Driven by the need to reduce costs and improve competitiveness, companies often reduce staffing costs. This is a common strategy, but problems arise when companies fail to capture critical knowledge from exiting employees. Downsizing can result in the exodus of valuable corporate knowledge assets. According to Dr. Carla O'Dell, president of the American Productivity and Quantity Center, cost-cutting and downsizing have resulted in a loss of knowledge for many organizations. One estimate asserts "that more than 450,000 years of experience have left . . . organizations as people take early retirement packages and leave."[18] Capturing the knowledge of departing managers has to be a critical priority for companies that are downsizing.

Information vs. Knowledge   The combination of poor knowledge management practices and the vast quantities of data generated by the conduct of business threaten

---

[16]Ivan Seidenberg's April 24, 1998, speech before the Massachusetts Software Council.

[17]October 29, 1997, speech before the Economic Club of Chicago.

[18]Susan Elliott, "APQC Conference Attendees Discover the Value and Enablers of a Successful KM Program," *Knowledge Management in Practice,* December 1996/January 1997.

to make companies information rich but knowledge poor. Knowledge management can convert these information streams into new sources of company value. The achievements and technical acumen of employees are critical links to competitive advantage in highly technical industries. Effective knowledge management can compensate for knowledge depletion and information overload by locating and tapping hidden reserves of knowledge within a company and augmenting these with low-cost internal and external resources such as intranets, extranets, and information systems and software.

To succeed in the new world order, companies must adopt a new conceptual framework, in which knowledge is treated as a core corporate asset rather than an expense. Investments in new information infrastructures alone will not ensure success. Equal attention must be given to identifying, creating, managing, and leveraging the knowledge assets needed to market, sell, bill, procure, maintain, and manage these tangible assets.

CONCLUSION

As companies move forward, they must negotiate difficult paths between serving existing markets within existing frameworks and developing new initiatives and frameworks to meet the challenge of new competitors and opportunities. The key to negotiating between these opposing forces successfully is knowledge—specifically the knowledge assets each firm holds within it.

Identifying knowledge assets is the difficult first task. Each asset must be evaluated for the contribution it makes to current and future revenue streams. This is a daunting task. These are only the first steps. Designing and implementing initiatives to manage, grow, and leverage knowledge assets to serve strategic visions is the next task. Effective knowledge management is the key to survival in the knowledge economy. Effective management requires measurement, tools, strategies, and vision. There is no turning back: Managers must embrace this future and learn how to manage their companies' knowledge assets.

But as with all new departures, we carry with us much of our past on the journey forward. It is not our intent to insist that the knowledge economy or "new economy" differs in all aspects from an "old economy." Many—perhaps most—basic economic and business principles will hold true for both economic models. Certainly in this case, a revolution need not destroy the past in order to assert its own validity. In short, the knowledge economy is a transition and development from previous economic models, and is best understood in that context.

QUESTIONS FOR REVIEW

1. How much of the knowledge-based economy is based on knowledge as a product/ service?

2. What are the bases for the electronic economy? What role will knowledge management play in this new environment?

3. What role does information technology infrastructure play in managing knowledge assets globally?

4. What are the new "rules" of this networked economy, and how will these rules affect knowledge management strategies?

5. How will the growing deficit in information technology workers and hyper-competition affect organizations' abilities to leverage knowledge assets?

6. How will the basis for investing in corporate assets change in the knowledge-based economy?

7. What will it take for individuals, as well as organizations, to succeed in this new world order?

CASE STUDY: Dell and the Internet

Dell Computer Corporation is a leading direct computer systems company. In the United States, Dell ranks number one and is a premier supplier of PCs to business customers, government agencies, educational institutions, and consumers. Dell's success has come from focusing on direct sales. While other companies ignored this channel, Michael Dell formed the company in 1984 with $1,000 of starting capital and no venture capital, forming what he refers to as the "direct business" model. In 1992, direct sales accounted for only 15 percent of PC sales, but by 1998 this sales method accounted for one-third of PC sales. Dell's PCs are built to order, and are enhanced by the knowledge the company gains from direct sales made in the past.

Dell has been able to succeed because it strives for quicker operations and lower overhead. Dell keeps inventory costs low by turning inventory over every seven days on average and can turn sales into cash in 24 hours compared to Compaq's average of 35 days. Dell is still improving its operations. The company has reduced the number of parts in a PC from 204 to 47 and has been working on speeding up delivery of these parts, moving selected distribution centers from Malaysia to Mexico.

However, all of these achievements pale in comparison to Dell's use of the Internet. Dell began selling PCs from the site www.dell.com in 1996 and recorded daily sales over the Internet of $50 million per day just four years later. The company set a goal in 1997 to have 50 percent of sales be over the Internet, and reached that goal by the end of the first quarter of 2000. This is an increase from $30 million per day over the past year.

However, Michael Dell does not see sales as the only value of the Internet. Direct contact with customers over the Internet helps keep inventory costs down and gives the company a competitive advantage. By having extensive knowledge of what the customer wants, money is not wasted on unpurchased inventory, crucial in the computer software industry where inventory value decreases about 1 percent per week. These savings allow Dell to sell their computers at 10 to 15 percent less than their rivals.

Dell's direct sales method has translated to success in the computer industry on- and off-line.

How has Dell leveraged knowledge and the new economic order to succeed? What must the management of Dell do to continue its success? How will their management of knowledge assets come into play?

3

PARADIGMS FOR KNOWLEDGE MANAGEMENT

The word *paradigm* is among the most overused words in the business lexicon except when used in combination with the word "shift." The notion of paradigms comes from philosopher of science Thomas Kuhn. In his highly regarded 1962 book *The Structure of Scientific Revolutions,* Kuhn described paradigms in the "mature" sciences of physics and chemistry.

Kuhn uses the word *paradigm* in various contexts, but the general theme can be likened to "point of view" or "world view." To use an analogy in religion, if one is a Christian, he/she has a world view based on the principle or fundamental assumptions set forth in the Christian Bible. For example, a Christian explanation of "God" will be based on the Christian paradigm.

A paradigm shift occurs when a fundamentally new understanding of a given phenomenon offers a more adequate or appealing explanation than the existing paradigm. The field of physics experienced a paradigm shift when Einsteinian physics supplanted Newtonian physics as a way of explaining subatomic particles and as a way of unifying the fields of energy and matter in his famous $e = mc^2$ equation.

Measurement is fundamental to scientific paradigms. The assumption that there is a fundamental or universal unit of measurement is a key feature of mature science. Any approach without a universal unit is less than a paradigm; it is "pretheoretic" or "prescientific." For example, the emerging paradigm of "dark matter" and "dark energy" in the universe depends directly on new *measurements,* particularly of super novae.

We employ the paradigm notion throughout this book because it provides a convenient way to frame the implications of fundamental shifts in thinking and subsequent management actions. Knowledge management will survive as a discipline to the extent that its theorists and practitioners commit to a basic unit of measurement and a common set of characteristics defining knowledge and its management.

Fundamental Assumptions

Paradigms offer sets of fundamental assumptions about the world and how it can be explained. For example, a Christian paradigm assumes that forgiving one's enemy is desirable. Other religious paradigms may not share this fundamental assumption. Similarly, the principles of "Scientific Management," prevalent in the early 20th century, assumed that:

- Organizations could be viewed as machines following scientific principles derived from Newtonian physics.
- People are just as replaceable as any other machine part in the organization.
- Work quotas can be based on scientific analysis of what outputs were possible for "human" machine parts.
- Controlling human behavior at work was the principal impediment to creating a perfectly functioning organizational "machine."

This management paradigm was subsequently replaced by the view of workers as a human resource.

Knowledge management has yet to reach paradigm status in Kuhn's sense of the term. No universal unit of knowledge has wide acceptance. However, several economic paradigms feature underlying assumptions upon which approaches to knowledge management can be formulated. For example, money is the principal unit in economics, and money is understood to be an abstract representation for underlying units of output such as products, services, and resources.

Just as products that could be resolved into atoms were the fundamental units of the Industrial Age, knowledge that can be resolved into bits is the fundamental unit of the Information Age.[1]

Both atoms and bits have coexisted for centuries. However, in the modern age, bits have provided the leverage or engine for economic growth. The quasi-paradigm shift from Industrial to Information Age brings with it a set of underlying assumptions that differ substantially. For example, in the Industrial Age the assumption of diminishing returns was fundamental and unquestioned. Today, however, the assumption of increasing returns provides a more satisfying explanation for an economy based on bits.[2]

This shift in our world view has created the need for new methods of measurement that are not based on the fundamental assumptions of the Industrial Age.[3] The existing ways of accounting for business phenomena will not suffice in this new paradigm. The new framework requires counting and recording bits, the fundamental unit of knowledge. Armed with this new framework and its underlying assumptions, managers can develop new ways to monitor, explain, and predict behavior in their organizations. This becomes the essential ingredient for how they conceptualize and manage their organizations. Old industrial-era assumptions routed in the mechanistic approach may blind managers to the opportunities offered by utilizing the assumptions of the Information Age.[4]

---

[1]Based on Shannon's information theory.

[2]See Brian Arthur's work on increasing returns published in various places including a recent *Harvard Business Review* article. July–August 1996, pp. 100–9.

[3]See R. K. Elliot's writings on this subject beginning with his formative article, "The Third Wave Breaks on the Shores of Accounting" published in *Accounting Horizons* in 1992.

[4]See Housel and Kanevsky's discussion of the "Thermodynamics of Business Processes" in "Reengineering Business Processes: A Complexity Theory Approach to Value Added," *INFOR*, 33, pp. 248–62.

Managers, like scientists, make decisions based on their fundamental understandings derived from the paradigms to which they subscribe. In the modern era, managing knowledge is the key to leveraging the economics of the modern age. As such, approaches to knowledge management must be developed within the context of the scientific paradigms that can be used to provide the grounding assumptions for the knowledge economy.

The Industrial Age is an aging business model that is being slowly replaced by the Information Age model. However, many managers still operate according to Industrial Age assumptions. This situation can be explained by one or both of the following reasons:

1. Managers simply choose not to change with the shift to the new paradigm.
2. Many managers employ business forms and practices that are highly optimized for traditional manufacturing.

Management in these companies essentially competes on price rather than on product differentiation, and they have been successful doing so.

In the industrial era, companies operated on assumptions rooted in tangible-assets-based explanations that basically tracked the physical transformations of atoms into finished goods in order to create wealth. Atoms represent the raw material used to create valued outputs. In this framework the Sultan of Brunei became one of the wealthiest individuals in the world by extracting petroleum atoms, or oil, that is eventually transformed into gasoline.

Companies competing under the old model tend to have highly standardized operational procedures for relatively simple products. Design and operational complexity, as well as customizability, is generally squeezed out of the production process. Examples of companies like these can be found in the commodity industries.

In the modern era based on knowledge, this approach can be suicidal because reverse-knowledge engineering enables competitors to produce the same processes/products easily. Personal computer manufacturing is a familiar example because components are based on defined common standards and companies readily produce commodity components. On the other hand, the PC software industry is a very different environment where Microsoft, Oracle, and SAP capture and reuse unique knowledge in the form of lines of code and in the methods to produce that code. As evidence of the shift in power from the Industrial to the Information Age, Bill Gates, CEO of Microsoft, is wealthier than the Sultan of Brunei.

According to some futurists, such as Eric Saffo, we are 10 years into the Information Age. Companies that are flourishing in this new age employ frameworks that recognize knowledge as a core asset that they use to produce and differentiate their products. Deploying these knowledge assets generates the value from which they profit. The lesson for investors and entrepreneurs is that differential leverage in the Information Age will come from the ability to capture and reuse valuable knowledge better than others.

Transforming bits into valued forms of knowledge serves as a virtual representation of all corporate outputs in our era. For the modern company, a bit is a virtual atom that is utilized as raw material to create finished goods. This is made possible by the use of information technology and telecommunications, which facilitate the manipulation and distribution of virtual outputs.

Microsoft, for example, ultimately creates value by compiling bits into programs. The primary engine of wealth is not the compact disc or manual. Wealth is created by selling new and reused computer code. Both old and new paradigms provide assumptions that allow managers to manage corporate assets. Critically, the assumptions governing the management of knowledge assets differ radically from those governing the management of industrial-era tangible assets. Managers from both perspectives would see a group of employees and machinery, but the inputs, processes, and outputs are viewed in radically different ways.

Information Age managers see a set of knowledge assets distributed among people, machines, and processes coordinated to produce desired outputs. Basic decisions are based on assumptions about the knowledge required to operate a given process and how it can be embedded in information technology to make it easily reusable. These managers also recognize that some knowledge assets are better left in the brains of employees. Their intellectual capital creates the leverage and flexibility to rapidly deploy new knowledge and create an ever-changing array of products and services. In this way, the critical problem for management is how to best introduce, utilize, and deploy knowledge throughout the company's core processes.

In contrast, Industrial Age managers see a company's core processes as piece parts of a machine operating in predetermined ways to yield a more or less consistent set of tangible outputs. Ensuring that the parts are interchangeable is a common goal. Embedding knowledge within machines and employing tightly defined job descriptions are common approaches. Supervision aims to ensure that employees behave within the well-defined limits, and managers believe that obtaining enough measures of the process will optimize the process. This seeing the "trees through the forest" approach is based on the reductionist assumptions of the industrial-era paradigm. Focusing on tangible outputs rather than on the knowledge assets deployed to produce the outputs is common practice.

Although both managers focus on the same tangible assets, the Information Age manager's paradigm leads to explicit management of intangible assets. The Industrial Age manager's paradigm does not provide a framework for managing the intangible assets he literally does not "see." The Information Age paradigm allows managers to "see" patterns, and the patterns that provide the most leverage in today's economy are based on knowledge.

The Information Age paradigm allows management to view knowledge as output. Used as a surrogate, knowledge provides a way for all companies to view their operations in terms of a knowledge-based framework. When companies view themselves as a set of knowledge assets and knowledge outputs, they can identify and invest in the processes, technologies, and people that provide the greatest return. This view facilitates a portfolio approach to the management of corporate knowledge assets and provides a new valuation tool for companies.

MEASUREMENT IS ESSENTIAL TO MANAGEMENT

It has been often stated that you cannot manage what you cannot measure. This notion has its roots in the understanding that a system requires feedback to keep it on track.

What managers measure determines what feedback they obtain and how well their systems are geared to achieving their goals.

The management of knowledge is no exception to this general rule. Managers must obtain feedback on how well their systems are utilizing the knowledge deployed therein. Approaches to measuring knowledge and its impacts on marketplaces and organizations can be characterized as

A. Process of elimination.
B. It's in here somewhere.
C. Everything is cost.
D. Rorschach.
E. Forget it.
F. Knowledge is proportionate to value.

Process of Elimination[5]

Baruch Lev's pioneering work on valuing the intellectual capital in companies follows the "process of elimination" approach to measuring the economic impacts of knowledge. This method estimates by subtracting the expected income from a firm's tangible and financial assets from past and expected earnings to give the company's "knowledge earnings." A discount rate is applied to the average posttax return for three knowledge-intensive industries (such as computer software) to obtain the company's "knowledge capital." In essence, this approach identifies the knowledge assets by subtracting the effect of all other assets. What is left over is assumed to be the knowledge asset.

This approach assumes that it is possible to separate tangible and intangible assets for analysis in isolation.

Similarly, Paul Strassmann proposes an aggregate level approach to measuring "knowledge capital." Knowledge capital is treated as a residual derived from filtering out the contributions of financial capital. This measure results from applying economic value-added (which is the true cost of capital, calculated by subtracting all economic costs, that is, land, cost of goods, taxes, shareholder compensation, and so forth from revenue) to derive the knowledge capital residual.

Strassmann's approach produces several other measures of the impact of knowledge on corporate performance:

- Knowledge accumulation.
- Knowledge capital valuation of employees.
- Contribution of information technology knowledge capital.

Strassmann summarizes his view of the value of measuring knowledge capital.

---

[5]In a sense, any approach that does not posit a "unit" level measurement for knowledge is a process-of-elimination approach. However, it is useful to characterize the general approaches to dealing with the issue of measuring knowledge, or its impact, to better understand the paradigm within which these kinds of approaches attempt to explain phenomena that they cannot "see."

The calculation of the Economic Value-Added makes it possible to count the worth of the people who possess the accumulated knowledge about a company. These are the carriers of Knowledge Capital. They are the people who leave the workplace every night and many never return while storing in their heads knowledge acquired while listening and talking while delivering nothing of tangible value to paying customers. Their brains have become repositories of an accumulation of insights about how "things work here"—something that is often labeled by the vague expression "company culture." Their heads carry a share of the company's Knowledge Capital, which makes them shareholders of Knowledge Assets. In fact they become managers, because information acquisition and information utilization is the essence of all managerial acts.

These process-of-elimination approaches target the aggregate level of analysis. They are of greatest interest to investors and senior executives who wish to benchmark their company's use of knowledge assets. Managers, however, might want to look directly at the company's knowledge assets deployed in specific core processes to see how they are performing before deciding how best to improve their performance.

Such approaches do not focus on a disaggregated, common, unit of measurement for the analysis of knowledge contributions within the organization. An important problem for such approaches is to measure the interaction of tangible and intangible assets as they jointly produce value in core processes. The ratio of value produced by each might prove a useful estimate of the company's knowledge leverage.

It's in Here Somewhere

Edvinsson and Malone measure intellectual capital with an "all-encompassing" reporting model. Theirs is the best representative of this approach. Their model has more than 140 indicators of intellectual capital and its derivatives. They assume that if enough aspects of intellectual capital can be captured, we will have a "complete" understanding of the phenomenon.

The indicators displayed in Table 3.1 are a sampling of the ones included in Edvinsson and Malone's model. Missing is a theoretical framework showing how the indicators are related. If we take the measures to be linear, we can add them up to generate an aggregate score. Unfortunately, it would require an incredibly complex mathematical algorithm to combine the indicators.

This approach may provide useful information on an indicator-by-indicator basis depending upon what the manager or investor is interested in knowing. Intellectual capital or knowledge assets are likely present somewhere in this set of indicators. For the manager, the problem is finding out which indicator(s) really matter.[6]

[6]See *Forbes ASAP* (April 1997) devoted to the issue of measuring intellectual knowledge management for a review of the problems with this approach. For example, John Rutledge makes the following comments: "He [Leif Edvinsson] and his colleagues at Skandia built a model that at last count had 164 different variables, not including subcategories, to explain and measure intellectual capital. It must have been a long night when they thought all those things up, because toward the end they had to use 'share of employees under age 40 (%),' 'number of women managers,' and 'average age of employees' to pad the list. I can't even imagine what they had in mind with those ideas. . . . If you want to measure the value of people and their ideas, you need to look at cash flows, not assets. Balance sheets measure the value of things you own; cash flows measure the value of things you rent. Unless we return to conditions in the antebellum South, this will remain true no matter how many computers we have on our desktops or how fast they run."

TABLE 3.1   MEASURES OF INTELLECTUAL CAPITAL

Financial	Customer
1. Total assets ($)	1. Market share (%)
2. Total assets/employee ($)	2. Number of customers (#)
3. Revenues/total assets (%)	3. Annual sales/customer ($)
4. Profits/total assets (%)	4. Customers lost (#)
5. Revenues resulting from new business operations ($)	5. Average duration of customer relationship (#)
6. Profits resulting from new business operations ($)	6. Average customer size ($)
7. Revenues/employee ($)	7. Customer rating (%)
8. Customer time/employee attendance (%)	8. Customer visits to the company (#)
9. Profits/employee ($)	9. Days visiting customers (#)
10. Lost business revenues compared to market average (%)	10. Customers/employee (#)
11. Revenues from new customers/total revenues (%)	11. Field salespeople (#)
12. Market value ($)	12. Field sales management (#)
13. Return on net asset value (%)	13. Average time from customer contact to sales response (#)
14. Return on net assets resulting from new business operations ($)	14. Sales closed/sales contacts (%)
15. Value added/employee ($)	15. Satisfied customer index (%)
16. Value added/IT employees ($)	16. IT investment/salesperson ($)
17. Investments in IT ($)	17. IT investment/service and support employee ($)
	18. Support expense/customer ($)
	19. Service expense/customer/year ($)
	20. Service expense/customer/contact ($)

Human	Renewal and Development
1. Leadership index (#)	1. Competence development expense/employee ($)
2. Motivation index (#)	2. Satisfied employee index (#)
3. Empowerment index (#)	3. Marketing expense/customer ($)
4. Number of employees (#)	4. Share of training hours (%)
5. Employee turnover (%)	5. Share of development hours (%)
6. Average employee years of service with company (#)	6. Employee's view (empowerment index) (#)
7. Number of managers (#)	7. R & D expense/administrative expense (%)
8. Number of women managers (#)	
9. Average age of employees (#)	8. Training expense/employee ($)
10. Share of employees less than 40 years old (%)	9. Training expense/administrative expense (%)
11. Time in training (days/year) (#)	10. Business development expense/administrative expense (%)
12. Number of directors (#)	11. Share of employees below age 40 (%)
13. Number of women directors (#)	12. IT development expense/IT expense (%)
14. Number of full-time or permanent employees (#)	13. IT expenses on training/IT expense (%)
15. Average age of full-time or permanent employees (#)	14. R & D resources/total resources (%)
16. Average years with company of full-time or permanent employees (#)	15. Customer base (#)
	16. Average customer age (#)

(continued on next page)

TABLE 3.1   MEASURES OF INTELLECTUAL CAPITAL *(continued)*

17. Annual turnover of full-time permanent employees (#)
18. Per capita annual cost of training, communication, and support programs for full-time permanent employees ($)
19. Full-time or permanent employees who spend less than 50% of work hours at a corporate facility (#)
20. Percentage of full-time permanent employees (%)
21. Per capita annual cost of training, communication, and support programs ($)
22. Number of full-time temporary employees (#)
23. Average years with company of full-time temporary employees (#)
24. Per capita annual cost of training and support programs for full-time temporary employees ($)
25. Number of part-time employees or non-full-time contractors (#), average duration of contract (#)
26. Company managers with advanced degrees: business (%), science and engineering (%), liberal arts (%)

17. Average customer education (#)
18. Average customer income ($)
19. Average customer duration with company (months) (#)
20. Training investment/customer ($)
21. Direct communications to customer/year (#)
22. Non-product-related expense/customer/year ($)
23. New market development investment ($)
24. Industry development investment ($)
25. Value of EDI system ($)
26. Upgrades to EDI system ($)
27. Capacity of EDI system (#)
28. Ratio of new products (less than 2 years old) to full company catalog (%)
29. Ratio of new products (less than 2 years old) to product family (%)
30. R & D invested in basic research (%)
31. R & D invested in product design (%)
32. R & D invested in processes (%)
33. Investment in new product support and training ($)
34. Average age of company patents (#)
35. Patents pending (#)

Process

1. Administrative expense/total revenues (%)
2. Cost for administrative error/management revenues (%)
3. Processing time, outpayments (#)
4. Contracts filed without error (#)
5. Function points/employee-month (#)
6. PCs/employee (#)
7. Laptops/employee (#)
8. Administrative expense/employee ($)
9. IT expense/employee ($)
10. IT expense/administrative expense (%)
11. Administrative expense/gross premium (%)
12. IT capacity [CPU and DASD] (#)
13. Change in IT inventory ($)
14. Corporate quality goal (#)
15. Corporate performance/quality goal (%)
16. Discontinued IT inventory/IT inventory (%)
17. Orphan IT inventory/IT inventory (%)
18. IT capacity/employee (#)
19. IT performance/employee (#)

Source: Adapted from Leif Edvinsson and Michael Malone, "Intellectual Capital," published by HarperCollins, New York, 1997, pp. 147–60.

Everything Is Cost

Activity-based costing (ABC) was not explicitly developed to measure the productivity of knowledge assets. However, costing models are widely accepted in accounting and management, and it is important to review the most prominent. ABC has both advantages and challenges in understanding the contributions of knowledge to corporate productivity. Since this approach has been widely applied, it likely will be applied to understand the contributions of knowledge to corporate productivity.

The everything-is-cost camp assumes that understanding the value of knowledge is simply a matter of calculating its cost or market price. The market price for one's knowledge is certainly one measure of its value for the knowledge holder, but it is a far stretch to say market price translates directly into the value that knowledge produces.

T. A. Stewart, author of the seminal book on intellectual capital, argued that there is no meaningful correlation between the cost of knowledge acquisition and knowledge value: "The value of intellectual capital isn't necessarily related to the cost of acquiring it."[7]

Activity-based costing focuses on finding the true cost of a given activity within a process. This methodology was explicitly developed to help manufacturers ascertain the true cost of producing their products.

There are numerous variations on the ABC approach. The following five steps are common to many.

FIVE STEPS TO ABC

---

1. Analyze Activities: Identify activities within processes; develop activity model (identify inputs, controls, outputs, and mechanisms); determine scope of project.
2. Gather Costs: Capture all relevant expenses that pertain to the selected processes and model.
3. Trace Costs to Activities: Costs identified in step 2 are assigned to their respective activities from step 1; resulting costs for each activity will represent resources used by that activity to convert inputs into outputs.
4. Establish Output Measures: Determine output measure for each activity; determine activity output costs per unit of output.
5. Analyze Costs: Culmination of all measurements and calculations occurred thus far; analyze and review all data to identify candidates for improvement.

Underlying all such cost-based approaches is the assumption that the most meaningful information about corporate processes can be derived from the costs they incur. With its roots in the Industrial Age paradigm, this approach would not allow a manager to "see" intangible assets such as knowledge. When managers nurtured on the Industrial Age paradigm approach the measurement of knowledge, they often attempt to derive its value based on some formulation of its cost. However, knowing the true cost of knowledge assets is difficult. Moreover, managers may assume that the most expensive

---

[7]T. A. Stewart, *Intellectual Capital: The New Wealth of Organizations* (New York: Doubleday, 1997), p. 173.

knowledge assets are the most valuable. Unfortunately, this would not lead the manager to actually see a "unit" of knowledge but rather would lead him/her to infer its value based on the cost of using the asset. Understanding the true cost to use a knowledge asset may be the most valuable use of ABC in calculating the performance of knowledge assets.

Rorschach Inkblot

Another set of approaches assumes that managers can derive the contribution of knowledge assets by viewing a family of intuitively related performance measures. While similar to "It's in Here Somewhere" approaches, these approaches are placed in their own category because they follow slightly different assumptions and usually employ very large numbers of indicators.

The actual nature of the relationship among the indicators is more a matter of what the individual manager believes, or via a consensus-gaining process, what a group of managers believes about the relationship among the measures. The Balanced Scorecard (Table 3.2) is most prominent among these approaches.

Balanced Scorecards focus on developing and monitoring strategy via a family of measures. They help translate corporate strategy into a set of goals and objectives, and their success is tracked through multiple performance measurements. As such, Balanced Scorecards aid in communication and in setting strategic objectives.

The Balanced Scorecard measures performance from at least four perspectives: learning and growth, internal processes, customer, and financial. Adequate investment in these areas is assumed to be critical to long-term success. Together, these four perspectives attempt to provide a balanced view of the present and future performance of the business.

In practice, scorecards typically have about five subscales for each perspective. The scales use ratio, interval, and ordinal approaches to capturing data about corporate per-

TABLE 3.2   BALANCED SCORECARD PERSPECTIVES

Perspective	Focus
The Learning and Growth Perspective	Directs attention to the organization's people and infrastructure.
The Internal Perspective	Focuses attention on the performance of the key internal processes that drive the business. Improvement in internal processes now is a key lead indicator of financial success in the future.
The Customer Perspective	Considers the business through the eyes of a customer, so that the organization retains a careful focus on customer needs and satisfaction.
The Financial Perspective	Measures the ultimate results that the business provides to its shareholders.

formance. Resulting scores are normalized to combine them into a single decision point. This approach assumes that the various measures are related to one another in a cause–effect chain linked to corporate strategy and the corporate bottom line. Developing a mathematical algorithm for the various measures within a consistent theoretical framework has proven to be difficult.

At present, users are left without a consistent mathematical explanation of the relations among the various scales, and interpretation is left to managers deciding how the measures should be related. This subjectivity relegates Balanced Scorecard approaches to the "prescientific" category, since there is no consistent theoretical framework. Observers are left to infer links between the bottom-line financial indicators and the other measures. Perhaps its most promising application is when it is used as a tool for communicating strategic intent.

Outputs Focus

A number of knowledge management thinkers believe that it is impossible to develop direct, meaningful measures of knowledge assets. Larry Prusak and Thomas Davenport are leading proponents of this point of view. They believe that it is possible to measure only the outputs of knowledge. Part of their dilemma results from the assumption that knowledge is by definition intangible and therefore unobservable. Members of this group infer that knowledge is responsible for outputs without identifying a common unit of output to be measured. They argue that outputs are enough and that the best we can hope for is measuring the impacts of knowledge. In defense of their position, exponents note that physicists confront the same problem in trying to measure and directly observe subatomic units. While quarks, for example, are unobservable, physicists still make reliable predictions about their behavior. Applying this approach to knowledge management fails to establish a specific relationship between the knowledge used and its presumed outputs. Positing a unit of knowledge would facilitate more reliable predictions about the utilization of knowledge assets and more complete explanations of how knowledge specifically contributes to organizational performance.

Knowledge Is Proportionate to Value

One may also assume that there is a direct relationship between knowledge and the value it creates.[8] Methodologies rooted in this approach are expressions of the Information Age framework and maintain that knowledge is directly observable and that specific units may be devised. This approach embodies a thermodynamics of knowledge within which common units of change within processes can be observed and measured.[9]

[8]See Kanevsky and Housel's discussion of the *Thermodynamics of Business Processes* and their reference to Cover and Thomas's proof, that an information theory bit is proportionate to a unit of "complexity" (complexity being the underlying unit that is describable as a unit of "knowledge"). Also see T. Cover and J. Thomas, "Elements of Information Theory" (New York: John Wiley, 1991).

[9]See Claude Shannon's extensive work on Information Theory.

Theorists of this school propose methodologies that aim to track the transformation of knowledge into valued outputs. In this approach, knowledge is not consumed when it is used to create value-adding changes. This position is bolstered by the performance of leading Information Age companies. For example, Microsoft has an estimated book value of approximately $13–20 billion, yet it has a market capitalization of $300–400 billion. This glaring differential represents the earning potential and the value of Microsoft's use of the knowledge embedded in its processes, technology, and people.

However, when we look at a classic industrial-era company like Bethlehem Steel Co. (BS), we find a book value of $1.2 billion, while it had a market value of $1.7 billion as of April 22, 1998. These values are very similar, because the accounting and market valuations closely correlate to the physical, tangible asset values.

So, how is it possible to identify the value embedded in these intangible assets? In the new model, knowledge becomes the fundamental asset to be measured. Understanding the transformation process of units of knowledge necessitates a core-process-level of analysis. Knowledge becomes the fundamental unit of measurement and must be tracked through processes. Because knowledge is intangible, we need a way to observe and describe how it adds value and how its use incurs cost.

As we move from the industrial to the knowledge economy, it becomes obvious that it will be very difficult to take our current accounting system with us.[10] Knowledge represents a surrogate for value, in addition to being a core, competitive asset. Drastic discrepancies in valuations of companies with minimal tangible assets, and the emergence of knowledge as a virtual asset, help substantiate this argument. Conventional accounting practices make no attempt to directly quantify and measure this knowledge.

Although the accounting community has been reluctant to accept nontraditional accounting methods, the identification, quantification, and accounting for knowledge assets is increasingly seen as critical for companies in the Information Age. Over the past several years a number of methodologies have emerged that may help companies in this mission-critical task. Many of these are still in the formative stages.

Knowledge value added (KVA) is an example of these approaches. KVA is a methodology designed to estimate the value of the knowledge deployed throughout a company's core processes. This is accomplished through a return ratio with the numerator of the ratio being the percentage of the revenue or sales dollar allocated to the amount of knowledge required to obtain the outputs of a given process in proportion to the total amount of knowledge required to generate the corporation's salable outputs. The denominator of the ratio is the cost to execute the process knowledge. The general notion can be best understood by a real example.

In this example of KVA, aggregated data was gathered over a month on a core process at a regional telecommunications company. The KVA analysts, using a workflow model of the process, interviewed process subject-matter experts, made observations, and talked with process employees and managers to obtain average learning

---

[10]R. K. Elliot, senior partner for KPMG and president of the American Institute of Certified Public Accountants, has written numerous articles in *Accounting Horizons* and made several videotapes on this very subject.

TABLE 3.3   KVA EXAMPLE

Outside Plant Provisioning Center

Sub-process	Learning time (months)	Value added ($)	Process instruc-tions	Value added ($)	Execution time (min)	Weekly rate ($)	Process costs ($)	ROK (%)	ROP (%)
Permit	301	1,026	278	264	5,550	628.00	1,452	71	18
CWBO	625	2,133	300	286	9,000	628.00	2,355	91	12
Status	500	1,706	2,750	2,617	33,000	628.00	8,635	20	30
Scheduling	9,000	30,716	37,000	35,212	20,500	661.00	5,646	544	624
Reproduction	125	427	2,750	2,617	15,000	628.00	3,925	11	67
Estimating	9,000	30,716	31,750	30,216	81,000	661.00	22,309	138	135
Posting	9,000	30,716	27,750	26,409	307,500	661.00	84,691	36	31
IT	750	2,560	2,500	2,379	100[a]	1,500.00	12,000	21	20
Sum	29,301	$100,000	105,078	$100,000			$141,013	71%	71%
Price	$100,000		$100,000						
Overall Return	3.41	Correlation	0.95						

[a]The execution time in minutes for the information systems that supported this core process was minimal, as one might expect with information technology. However, the cost to maintain the systems was rather high, resulting in the average $120-per-minute execution time cost.

time[11] estimates and the number of roughly equivalent process instructions (in terms of the complexity to learn them) required to complete each subprocess.

Comparing the Permit subprocess to the Estimating subprocess, for example, makes it clear that estimating provided a better return on knowledge (138% versus 71%). That is, the amount of knowledge executed during the month was significantly higher in the Estimating subprocess than in the Permit subprocess, given the cost required to execute the knowledge. The Estimating process also was significantly more costly. However, since KVA provides a performance ratio estimate, it is also possible to see that this sub-process provided a much higher return on knowledge.

In this way, KVA led the manager of this core process to think about how knowledge could be managed to produce better returns. If managers focused only on cost rather than the value of the knowledge in the process, they would have only one option—cut costs. However, if they cut costs in the Estimating subprocess without maintaining the same output level, they would actually be reducing the return on this subprocess. KVA standardizes the output of all processes by describing the output in terms of the units of knowledge required to produce the output.

---

[11]Using the same person as a reference point, on average, the time it takes to learn a predefined process is proportionate to the amount of knowledge required to execute the process correctly.

CONCLUSION

The impact of the paradigm shift from the Industrial Age to Information Age cannot be underestimated let alone understood without recognizing that this shift has also resulted in a new set of assumptions about how to describe, explain, and predict the behavior of organizations. The new paradigm has helped management theorists generate new theoretical frameworks to observe, measure, and manage intangibles such as knowledge. Attempting to take advantage of the opportunities that such new understandings afford, managers will continue to be inhibited by their reluctance to seek new measures of corporate performance, relying instead on the old indicators derived from the raw data of industrial-era economic theories.

The new paradigm allows managers to view knowledge as an asset that can be observed, measured, and managed. This paradigm shift allows managers to posit equivalent units of knowledge and the ability to link them to the bottom line. Some simple rules of thumb can be summarized that will help managers better leverage this new understanding:

- Posit a common unit of knowledge based on some theoretical framework that is consistent with the new paradigm.
- The value of a unit of knowledge is not necessarily equivalent to its cost.
- Recognize that all observation is "subjective" because it is made within the context of a paradigmatic point of view.
- Valid observations can only be made from a consistent theoretical framework within the context of a given paradigm.

Selection of a measurement approach to aid in managing knowledge will be based in large part on the underlying paradigm managers use to view their companies' processes. Those that see their core processes primarily as necessary costs that must be reduced and simplified will likely select a cost-based methodology such as ABC. Those that see their core processes as portfolios of knowledge assets that must be employed to produce value will likely use a knowledge valuation approach such as KVA. Those that choose to rely on their creativity in interpreting multiple performance measures to understand how well corporate strategy is meeting a given set of objectives will likely choose an approach such as the Balanced Scorecard approach. Each approach carries with it a basic set of assumptions, and managers must review these assumptions to determine whether they are consistent with their own assumptions about how best to manage knowledge assets.

QUESTIONS FOR REVIEW

1. What is a paradigm?
2. What effect does a manager's paradigm have on his or her management and performance measurement for core processes?
3. What caused the paradigm shift from the Industrial to Information Age?

4. How can managers leverage the new paradigm to improve strategy and corporate performance?
5. What are the promises and challenges of the various ways to measure corporate knowledge asset performance?
6. Select one of the approaches and apply it to the management of Microsoft's core knowledge assets.
7. What is the difference between a scientific and prescientific approach?
8. What management advantages come from positing a common unit of knowledge?

CASE STUDY: Hughes Space and Communications

Under the direction of Arian Ward, the leader of Hughes's knowledge management project, Hughes has adapted an approach that minimizes costs and overhead often created by formalized programs. According to Ward, "We're trying to avoid top management support. As a matter of fact, I've asked them not to give it." He believes that employees will be far more likely to embrace new knowledge management practices if they are presented as something voluntary. "The whole idea is to get people involved in this because they care about it and they are interested in it—not because management tells them to do it. People are not completely resistant to change. What they are resistant to is being changed."[12]

With this in mind, Ward has begun to create "lessons learned" databases that are available to Hughes's various business units through groupware technology. He calls it a "knowledge highway." The goal is sharing new processes and practices throughout the organization so that each group can customize corporate knowledge to fit its particular needs. With an accent on information technology, he is creating "a common environment" in which knowledge can be easily transferred and new practices adopted freely.

In practice, the new environment has enabled Hughes engineers engaged in the fabrication of communications satellites to exchange insights about technology and process with other technicians, thereby cutting development time. Such exchanges are recorded and made available to help others involved in similar projects. By leveraging knowledge in this way, the manufacturing process can be perpetually enhanced to maintain a competitive edge. Ward says that Hughes must create the capabilities that enable employees to "rapidly and continuously learn."

The impetus for introducing knowledge management to Hughes was principally twofold. According to Ward, "the markets for government and commercial satellites were rapidly changing, prices were dropping faster than ever before, and we had to find a good way to get and use market intelligence." In addition, the company had been "downsizing and restructuring, and we're moving away from a federation of programs

---

[12]Britton Manasco, "Leading Companies Focus on Managing and Measuring Intellectual Capital," *Knowledge Inc.,* 1997, pp. 1–5: http://www.wbcom.com/quantera/.

to an integrated satellite factory. We needed better use of knowledge so we could stop repeating mistakes and stop reinventing."[13]

The Hughes example demonstrates that knowledge management practices can be successful when initiated from the bottom up. Ward's approach to introducing and implementing knowledge management initiatives has important implications for the ways managers should pursue their own knowledge management initiatives. Clearly, he was not working from existing approaches and frameworks for initiating and implementing new programs at Hughes.

For discussion: Over time, when should managers use the bottom-up or top-down practice, and what is the best way to introduce the new knowledge management practice? What paradigm was Ward working within when he developed his approach to knowledge management? How did Ward change the conceptual framework for management with his approach to knowledge management? Do you believe his is the best way given the many options available?

[13]Laurie Payne, "Unlocking an Organization's Ultimate Potential Through Knowledge Management," *Knowledge Management in Practice*, 1997: http://www.apqc.org/practice3.htm/.

4

KNOWLEDGE MANAGEMENT PRINCIPLES

If definitions can be thought of as the *description* of a product, principles are its *user's manual.* How-to principles emerge not only from intrinsic qualities of knowledge management ("how things should be") but also from trial-and-error best practices. Like a foundation being shored up and reinforced under a rapidly expanding building, the principles of knowledge management are being invented in part as companies experience their benefit.

This chapter recounts some of these experiences and extracts several constants of knowledge management that appear to hold across industries. In any emerging field, the tendency toward multiplicity of principles gradually gives way to singleness of vision and what Einstein called "elegance." Whether one enumerates a dozen or a hundred underlying principles of knowledge management, the intellectual thrust of all such effort is to locate and understand the mainsprings that set all the other gears into motion. In this context, this chapter asks the reader to reflect on knowledge management principles.

> *Knowledge has become the preeminent economic resource—more important than raw material; more important, often, than money. Considered as an economic output, information and knowledge are more important than automobiles, oil, steel, or any of the products of the Industrial Age.*[1]

In today's Information Age economy, knowledge is increasingly regarded as the preeminent contributor to value creation across industrial and service landscapes. The collection of information has always been of interest and value to companies. However, it is the emergence of tools that enable companies to manage and leverage their information and knowledge in meaningful ways that has engendered revolutionary change in the way knowledge is regarded. Unfortunately, the ability to manage and leverage knowledge has led to a proliferation of knowledge management approaches, measurement tools, initiatives, definitions, and procedures. This proliferation has created confusion and inhibits companies from reaching their desired destination. This chapter

---

[1]Thomas A. Stewart, *Intellectual Capital: The New Wealth of Organizations,* 1997, p. 6.

focuses on knowledge management principles in an effort to create a common ground for understanding this critical corporate activity.

KNOWLEDGE MANAGEMENT OVERVIEW

Companies in a wide variety of industries have launched knowledge management initiatives. According to leading practitioners in the field, the potential impact of knowledge management on the national and global economy is immense. International Data Corporation (IDC) believes that the market impact of knowledge management will be analogous to that of the Internet.[2] The firm makes the following primary points:

- Knowledge management will be a catalyst for many information technology (IT) product and service markets.
- Knowledge management will allow companies to establish exclusive market niches.
- Knowledge management will be an integral enhancement for many existing offerings.

According to IDC, the U.S. knowledge management consulting market in 1998 was valued at $1.1 billion; by 2000 it was predicted to be $1.9 billion, and by 2002 it is expected to be $3.4 billion. Similarly, according to the Gartner Group, U.S. businesses paid $1.5 billion to consultants for knowledge management advice in 1996. They are expected to pay $5 billion for it by 2001.

As significant as these numbers are, the knowledge management area is not clearly defined or understood, even by the primary players in the field. Many regard knowledge management as an enigma, with no one approach clearly explaining its elements. However, there is agreement on some of the principal difficulties associated with designing and implementing knowledge management practices:

- Culture change can be painful and exceptionally slow.
- Investment in necessary tools can be tenuous, incremental.
- Knowledge management is a high-level solution sell.
- A wall of confusion about knowledge measurement inhibits growth.

This last point is perhaps the most daunting. Most practitioners of knowledge management assessments have focused on qualitative issues; few have employed reliable measurement tools or applied rigorous quantitative analysis to the clients' processes.

Regardless of the difficulties, companies are beginning to realize the extraordinary benefits that can be gained from the implementation of knowledge management programs. For example, automakers Chrysler, Ford, and General Motors all have aggressive knowledge management initiatives under way. Petroleum and chemical companies Amoco, Dow, and Monsanto are implementing knowledge management practices. Companies as diverse as health care company Columbia/HCA Healthcare Corp. and clothing maker Fruit of the Loom, Ltd., have embraced the movement.

---

[2]See IDC's website, www.idc.com, for the latest knowledge management research from the company.

Knowledge management offers opportunities for companies to:

- Capture and analyze corporate information and apply it strategically in the form of data warehousing and data mining, decision support systems, and executive information systems.
- Create processes for worldwide access to information, enabling employees to make faster, more informed, and better decisions through intranets, groupware, and group decision support systems.
- Leverage the accumulated knowledge of past experiences across the company.
- Develop and complete projects with improved speed, agility, and safety.

Table 4.1 summarizes the initiatives currently undertaken by companies around the world.

KNOWLEDGE MANAGEMENT AND VALUE CREATION

Companies making the investment in knowledge management can realize huge bottom-line benefits. Those neglecting to do so can suffer tremendous costs in terms of lost revenues, customers, and markets. Consider the significant tangible benefits realized by the following companies:

- Chevron realized a $170 million annual savings by pooling and sharing knowledge that had been scattered and localized in various offices around the world. One team saved $150 million by sharing ways to reduce the use of electric power and fuel. Another team saved $20 million by comparing data on gas compressors.
- Dow Chemical increased its annual licensing revenues by $100 million by strategically managing its patents and licenses.

TABLE 4.1   KNOWLEDGE MANAGEMENT INITIATIVES

External structure initiatives	Internal structure initiatives	Competency initiatives
Gain knowledge from customers.	Build knowledge-sharing culture.	Create careers based on knowledge management.
Offer customers additional knowledge.	Create new revenues from existing knowledge.	Create microenvironments for tacit knowledge transfer.
	Capture individuals' tacit knowledge, store it, spread it, and reuse it.	Learn from simulations and pilot installations.
	Measure knowledge-creating processes and intangible assets.	
Companies: Benetton, General Electric, National Bicycle, Netscape, Ritz Carlton, Agro Corp., Frito-Lay, Dow Chemical, Skandia, Steelcase	*Companies: 3M, Analog Devices, Boeing, Buckman Labs, Chaparral Steel, Ford Motor Co., Hewlett-Packard, Chevron, British Petroleum, Telia, Celemi, Skandia*	*Companies: Buckman Labs, IBM, Pfizer, Hewlett-Packard, Honda, Xerox, National Technological University, Matsushita*

Source: Karl Sveiby, "What Is Knowledge Management?" at http://www.sveiby.com.au/knowledgemanagement.html.

- Booz Allen & Hamilton saves over $7 million a year by reducing the time needed to find and access employee and collaborative information.
- Silicon Graphics improved its Product Information Communication process and reduced annual sales-training costs from $3 million to $200,000.
- Steelcase experienced an upswing in patent applications and a threefold increase in productivity after implementing knowledge-sharing processes across multidisciplinary customer teams.

Ernst & Young believes that up to 80 percent of a company's resident knowledge is not being applied to business processes in a systematic, companywide manner. With knowledge widely dispersed throughout an organization, ways to access and manage knowledge must be organized in meaningful and useful ways. While many companies excel at collecting data, few have systematic processes for using that data. Fewer still have processes supported by the right culture and technologies to convert internal, employee-based information into value creating knowledge assets.

It is clear that knowledge management is emerging as the critical strategic activity. Unfortunately, it is also clear that a consolidated approach to interpreting, implementing, and applying knowledge management principles has yet to emerge. This is as true of companies operating within the information technology world as of those operating in the broader economy.

Knowledge management should be seen as a remedy for earlier attempts at "reengineering" rather than its latest version. Knowledge management's focus on identifying and maximizing knowledge value creation stands in sharp contrast to the "slash-and-burn" techniques associated with many reengineering strategies. Indeed, many of the reengineering efforts of companies have led to downsizing efforts that have actually cut huge swaths out of the knowledge base of these companies. Many are now struggling to repair the damage that resulted.

For example, several years ago a large Regional Bell Operating Company (RBOC) attempted to downsize the number of service representatives. The primary rationale for the reduction in staff was that this segment accounted for the largest overall costs because there were more service representatives than any other job category in the company. In terms of standard reengineering strategies, it seemed justified to reduce personnel from strictly a cost point of view. On the other hand, a knowledge audit conducted for the company quantitatively established that the service representatives' knowledge provided the highest return in the entire sales-order-provisioning process.

Despite this evidence, the number of service representatives was significantly reduced in downsizing efforts. The result was a two-month period of havoc while the company struggled to train new people. Knowledge was lost, revenues declined, and costs increased. The final result was a reduction in the company's ability to compete and less customer loyalty.

THE STATE OF KNOWLEDGE MANAGEMENT

Research into knowledge management reveals interesting anecdotal evidence and varied literature on current methodologies, techniques, tools, and case studies.

- Numerous and conflicting definitions of knowledge management.
- Wide diversity of implementation strategies with many companies in disparate industries engaged in knowledge management initiatives.
- No comprehensive understanding of the best techniques for designing and launching knowledge management initiatives.
- Very few detailed case studies of corporate experiences with knowledge management and knowledge gaps.
- Restricted access to information on how companies have resolved specific problems; this is primarily available at industry conferences on knowledge management.
- Ad hoc and noncomprehensive discussion of the techniques for measuring the value of knowledge management.
- Unclear links between knowledge asset utilization and financial results.
- General confusion about the difference between information retrieval and knowledge management.

WHY IS KNOWLEDGE MANAGEMENT IMPORTANT?

Knowledge management is crucial because it points the way to comprehensive and clearly understandable management initiatives and procedures. When companies fail to utilize tangible assets, they suffer the economic consequences, and this failure is clearly observable to markets and competitors alike. Although knowledge assets are harder to quantify, they are just as critical for the long-term survival and growth of the company.

We believe that success in today's competitive marketplace depends on the quality of knowledge and knowledge processes those organizations apply to key business activities. For example, maximizing the efficiency of the supply chain depends on applying knowledge of diverse areas such as raw materials sources, planning, manufacturing, and distribution. Likewise, product development requires knowledge of consumer requirements, recent scientific developments and new technologies, and marketing.

Deployment of the knowledge assets to create competitive advantage becomes even more crucial as:

- The marketplace becomes increasingly competitive and the rate of innovation continues to rise; knowledge must evolve and be assimilated at an ever faster rate.
- Corporations (re)organize business units to create customer value, and staff and management functions are redirected. As a result, there is a strong push to replace informal staff policies with formalized methods to align processes with customers.
- Competitive pressures reduce the size of the workforce that holds corporate knowledge. These pressures include increased employee mobility and early retirement, and they all lead to a loss of corporate knowledge.
- Employees have less and less unstructured time in which to acquire knowledge.
- Technologies increase complexity by allowing small operating companies to link with suppliers into transnational sourcing operations.

Restructuring often results in changes in strategic direction and in the loss of knowledge in specific functional areas. Subsequent reversals may create demand for the lost knowledge, but the essential employees with that knowledge may be long gone. Effective knowledge management initiatives can help eliminate the need for drastic restructurings as they help companies evolve with the changing economic environment. They can also help capture knowledge assets that would otherwise be lost due to necessary restructurings, retirement, and departing employees. This in turn can result in increased revenues, increased customer satisfaction and loyalty, enhanced competitive standing, and the ability to respond easily to changing market conditions. In this sense, knowledge management is as critical for companies in the Information Age as the assembly line and production management were in the Industrial Age.

PRACTICAL PRINCIPLES FOR MANAGING KNOWLEDGE

Theorists and practitioners alike are struggling to find a common set of principles to apply in successfully managing knowledge. Principles have been categorized according to how to create, collaborate, disseminate, reuse, embed, store, monitor, and measure knowledge to meet a variety of organizational goals. The principles have been derived from practice, theory, and various combinations of the two.

The following list is by no means exhaustive or generally agreed upon. However, the principles provide basic guidance for those attempting to develop new ways of managing knowledge assets. Customer knowledge, deploying knowledge in information technology, and monitoring and measuring knowledge assets are the places where knowledge management principles can be practically applied.

Customer Knowledge

The first set of principles aims to lower transaction costs, increase the volume of transactions, and improve customer satisfaction. These outcomes are accomplished by embedding customer knowledge and fail-safeing the transaction process.

1. Identify the knowledge that customers really value and make sure it is deployed in products, services, and self-service opportunities.

Following this principle would lead the manager to ask how much knowledge a customer employs in completing a transaction with the company. For example, an "e-tailer" such as eToys has created a transaction process where the customer visits their website and uses the company Web interface to obtain a desired toy, seek suggestions, find out what others have purchased, or to review the company's toy inventory.

By visiting the company website, the customer becomes a part of the transaction process by activating the knowledge embedded in company sales, order, provisioning, and production software.

The customer-activated knowledge costs the company next to nothing, as long as the site is well designed. Costs are incurred only if the site interface is so bad that customers make errors requiring human intervention in the form of call center support, rework with suppliers, system failures, or bad debt collection. A site with a robust technology platform also allows a very large number of customers to complete transactions at the same time. The benefits of having customers activate transaction process knowledge, cost savings, and virtually unlimited transaction capacity are possible only when the customer interface prevents them from making errors and is so appealing to the customer that customers will return time and time again.

To prevent customer-induced errors, company interfaces must facilitate customers' self-service without generating errors. One method is to use the notion of "e-Poke-Yoke."[3] The concept of mistake-proofing or Poke-Yoke originated in Japanese manufacturing practice, and Dick Chase adapted the principles and practices for the service sector. "Mistake-proofing is a powerful and comprehensive method for eliminating mistakes and defects, ensuring quality products and services."[4]

Customer errors can take place in three stages of a service encounter: preparation, encounter, and resolution.

1. Mistakes in the *preparation* for the encounter occur when customers fail to[5]
   a. bring necessary information or materials to the encounter (transaction).
   b. understand and anticipate their roles in the service transaction.
   c. engage the correct service.
2. Mistakes in the *encounter* arise from failure to
   a. remember steps in the service process.
   b. follow system flow.
   c. specify desires sufficiently.
   d. follow instructions.
3. Mistakes in the *resolution* of the encounter occur from failure to
   a. signal service failures.
   b. learn from the experience.
   c. adjust expectations appropriately.
   d. execute appropriate postencounter actions.

Understanding the likely points of failure in a customer service encounter can be applied to design principles for Web-based interfaces.

The interface designer should attempt to determine where customer-induced mistakes are most likely to happen and institute warnings or controls to prevent them. Six types of cues that are used to mistake-proof systems have previously been identified by scholars:[6]

- Warnings—the system merely indicates that a mistake has been made, and then continues with normal activity.
- Gagging—a mistake causes the system to grind to a halt until the mistake is cleared and the system restarted.

---

[3]The notion of "e-Poke-Yoke" was a collaboration of Dick Chase and the authors. Dr. Chase is the leading world expert in applying the principles and practices of Poke-Yoke to the service area.

[4]Richard B. Chase and Douglas M. Stewart, *Mistake-Proofing: Designing Errors Out* (Portland, OR: Productivity Press, 1995), p. 2.

[5]Ibid., pp. 11–12.

[6]C. Lewis and D. Norman, "Designing for Error," in *User Centered System Design,* ed. D. Norman and S. W. Draper (Hillsdale, NJ: Lawrence Erlbaum Associates, 1986), pp. 411–32.

- Nonresponse—the system does not respond at all to a mistake and does not accept the input.
- Self-correct—the system signals that a mistake was made and suggests a similar correct response.
- Talk about it—the system opens a dialog in order to reach an agreement about what is really intended.
- Teach me—the system learns the intentions associated with the mistaken actions and delivers the intended results if these same incorrect actions are performed in the future.

Putting these types of cues in the context of embedding customer knowledge within the interface offers some interesting possibilities. A general principle derived from this previous work is that a customer should only be given options consistent with his/her personalized knowledge, previously embedded in the interface. For example, a travel service interface for businesspeople might embed the traveler's company's guidelines for predetermined air carrier, class of service, hotel chain, and meal costs, as well as the customer's preferences for travel times, mode of transportation, and airports. When the customer selects an air carrier not approved by his/her company, the customer is warned. Another possibility is to have the interface "talk about it" with the customer, asking if the customer really intended to select the unapproved carrier and "self-correct" by suggesting a company-approved carrier.

Pushing these cues a bit further, the interface could provide a virtual travel counselor to actually "talk about it." The virtual counselor would provide a wider range of options for travel than had previously been established by the customer. If the customer had encountered a similar travel problem before, the interface could remind the customer how he/she overcame the problem last time. It could also display how other travelers from his/her company dealt with the problem successfully. As more and more person-alized customer knowledge is embedded in the company interface, these cues can provide a starting point for designing a mistake-proof interface over time.

Another principle to follow in providing self-service opportunities for e-customers is to embed as much intelligence in the company interface as is required to achieve a given set of transaction process goals. For example, online game interfaces provide players with enough information to have them take the lead in engaging others in competitive games. They do not struggle with the problems of reading and interpreting rules, knowing when to take turns, keeping score, posting results, or starting a new game. These interfaces are designed to allow the customers to engage in the "fun" of playing without having to struggle with the knowledge required just to get started.

Many e-tailer company interfaces are neither knowledge intensive nor customer enticing. They force the customer to use the same amount of knowledge required for a standard transaction with a brick-and-mortar retailer. However, superior interfaces that embed customer knowledge within the transaction process on a personalized basis can lead to faster and more satisfying transactions. Given the sad state of sales and customer support at many traditional retailers, the e-tailers have an opportunity to provide superior service.

Applying the customer-knowledge-embedding principle requires interfaces that make maximum use of customer knowledge in completing the transaction process. Several points to consider in designing a superior customer interface include:

- The time an average customer is willing to spend activating transaction knowledge.
- The amount of knowledge a customer will employ before losing interest.
- How much value is added each time they execute knowledge.

The goal here is to find the optimal upper and lower limits within these constraints and develop an interface that:

- Reduces the time a customer needs to complete the transaction process.
- Reuses a customer's knowledge by embedding it in the transaction process.
- Ensures that valued is added for the customer each time they execute knowledge in the transaction process.

Successful embedding of customer knowledge in more personalized interfaces will reduce the time required to complete the transaction process. The ongoing acquisition and embedding of customer knowledge will also create a "learning" interface that will continually be personalized for each customer.

A further step in providing customer value occurs when customers can compare their transaction behavior to that of others. These opportunities for social comparison meet customers' needs for reviewing their decisions, gaining support for their decisions, seeking advice, and maintaining inclusion in their perceived social groups.

The social comparison is facilitated by the use of collaborative filters, which compare user input with that of other users. For example, movie ratings and CD purchases can be tabulated to generate composite scores and recommend purchases of popular items; such decision-support capabilities built into company interfaces increases their perceived value for customers.[7]

Personalized knowledge may be obtained from customers during their introductions to the interface by:

- Providing some type of financial incentives, such as lower prices or discounts.
- Using Web-based client-server technologies to track browser behavior.

At a standard bricks-and-mortar retailer, salespeople capture the same consumer knowledge. They keep it in their heads, on paper files, and in other information systems. Sales representatives are using customer relationship management (CRM) systems to support such activities in the business-to-business marketplace. Improvements in these systems incorporate personalized customer knowledge so that customers will be able to employ more and more of the knowledge required to complete a transaction by themselves.

The relationship between customer knowledge and the amount of transaction process knowledge employed is portrayed in Figure 4.1. The more customer knowledge

---

[7]Current software products on the market include, for example, Likeminds and Net Perception.

FIGURE 4.1   Customer-Transaction Knowledge

embedded in the transaction process, the more transaction knowledge customers employ. This generally makes customers happier because it increases their control over the process.

Figure 4.2 demonstrates the relationship between the amount of customer knowledge embedded in a transaction process and the speed with which it takes place. As more customer-specific knowledge is embedded in a transaction process, it operates faster because customers don't have to work as hard at navigating and decision making through the process.

Company interfaces designed to increase customer-fired knowledge reduce the time required to execute transactions because of customer knowledge reuse and integration within the transaction process.

A random comparison of companies doing business in the Internet marketplace will provide examples of interfaces that have been designed with varying levels of "fail-safeing" and customer knowledge embedding.

FIGURE 4.2   Amount of Embedded Knowledge and Transaction Speed

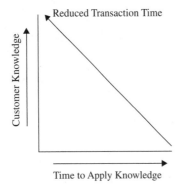

Many traditional companies do not employ the principles of fail-safeing and do not train service workers to answer customer questions about products and service. They also fail to create electronic interfaces that embed such knowledge, and will be doomed to failure over the long haul. The more aggressive retailers are moving rapidly to provide various forms of electronic customer interfaces via the Internet and kiosks within stores.

The benefits of incorporating customer knowledge via the company interface are many:

- Customer perception of more control over the transaction process.
- Closer bonding with customers.
- Lower company transaction costs.
- Greater volume of transactions per time period.

Appealing interfaces empower customers to do as much self-service as possible. The key to success is building interfaces, electronic and human, that deploy as much knowledge as customers need and want, to make the transaction process satisfying.

2. Make sure the customer product description and company description are as close as possible.

Customers expect that products and services will match their descriptions. Knowledge-based descriptions can be used to ensure that they are delivered as specified. The knowledge required to produce the product or service can be used to ensure that customers and providers have the same product description.

This is especially true for business-to-business transactions. Outsourcing decisions are common, and decisions are predicated on the belief that the outsourced services are delivered as specified.

Similarly, customers use lists of ingredients, fat content, calories per serving, FDA certifications, and so forth as guides for believing that they are getting a food product as specified. Brand names often serve as a surrogate for products and services that meet the customer's expectations, and the knowledge required to make them.

Over time, customers have become more discerning and look for more than brand names. For example, products and services that are assumed to be of high quality must meet customer expectations for performance over time. Given that it takes more knowledge to build a high-quality than a low-quality product or service, there should be a difference in the description of each. Companies can use this principle to guide their advertising, requirements for outsourcers, and production processes to ensure that the knowledge required to produce a high-quality product/service has actually been applied.

Knowledge and IT

Getting technology to do the work of humans has been the Holy Grail of the Information Age. Deciding what human work to move to information technology has been debated since the introduction of computers in the early 1950s. We believe the essence of the problem is deciding what human knowledge to deploy in information technology (IT). In general the more complex the knowledge is, the harder it is to deploy in IT.

Moving knowledge assets to IT offers a host of advantages if two basic principles are followed.

1. Move simple, procedural knowledge that is employed frequently to IT.

The focus of early automation efforts followed this principle as companies developed file-processing systems to do much of the tedious work in accounting, billing, and basic manufacturing. Since this knowledge is employed frequently and follows very specific, well-defined rules, moving it to IT allowed companies to dramatically lower the cost per use of the knowledge.

IT systems have advanced over time, making it easier to embed procedural knowledge that is activated frequently. The latest attempt to follow this principle can be found in enterprise resource planning (ERP) software from companies such as SAP, People-Soft, Baan, JD Edwards, and Oracle. These systems have succeeded largely where they have stuck to this principle. They have fallen down where they have attempted to tackle more complex knowledge or knowledge that is used infrequently. For example, attempts to use an ERP system at Hewlett-Packard Labs failed largely because the system attempted to embed engineering knowledge.[8] Several studies on Nova Corporation and CBPO found that attempts to automate simple knowledge that was used infrequently resulted in costs that far exceeded those of leaving the knowledge in human operators' heads and hands.

This embed simple and often used knowledge principle has guided IT efforts for several decades, but the new Internet-based IT offers opportunities to go a step further. For example, there is no reason that business-to-business system interfaces should not be personalized. All participants in a supply chain could take advantage of the customer-knowledge-embedding principle. Internet-based interfaces offer the opportunity to move the application of simple knowledge to supply chain partners. In time, even more complex formal knowledge could be embedded in transactional interfaces. Doing so extends good customer self-service to business partners and consequently offers excellent opportunities for further cost efficiencies throughout the supply chain.

2. Capture and embed knowledge in IT that is volatile and might be lost when employees leave the company.

When employees leave a company, they often take with them knowledge that is critical to continued smooth operations. It may not be possible to always capture complex employee knowledge. For example, Internet start-up companies are at the mercy of their technical employees whose heads contain the kind of complex knowledge necessary to build and grow a technical platform that will allow the company to rapidly expand.

In one case, the business development executive of an Internet start-up company described his strategy for dealing with this issue as "a knowledge redundancy strategy: two key technical employees for every key technical job." His company hired two

---

[8]Communication with Keith Stanton, former executive with HP.

employees for every area where critical technical knowledge was required. Given venture capitalists' demands for nearly immediate and continued growth, technical failure was not allowable. This is a rational approach because such complex knowledge is not in ready supply in the employment marketplace and is nearly impossible to embed in IT. However, the management realized that its long-term sustainability depends on capturing and embedding critical technical knowledge in less volatile forms such as IT and is currently moving to do so.

The field of artificial intelligence supports this general principle and has spawned expert systems and neural networks. Many of the earliest commercial attempts to embed complex knowledge in IT systems were based on what would be lost when "experts" in well-defined areas retired or left the company. Neural networks use an inductive approach, learning from the patterns that evolve from the behaviors of quasi-animate objects such as electronic ant colonies.

Groupware systems have attempted to capture critical complex knowledge assets so that they can be indexed and reused by others in a company. Many of the large consulting firms such as Arthur Andersen and Ernst & Young use groupware systems like Lotus Notes for just this purpose. Ernst & Young has a system named Ernie that allows clients to "ask Ernie" when they confront problems involving relatively complex consulting knowledge.

Intelligent agents embed complex knowledge that can be used for a variety of specific tasks. A variety of such agents embed knowledge used to meet specific goals and are reviewed in Chapter 8.

As information technology advances allow for greater embedding of complex human knowledge, they will provide a way to capture and reuse critical employee knowledge. However, until someone discovers the algorithm for creativity, it is unlikely that all employee knowledge will be amenable to embedding in IT.

Monitoring and Measuring Knowledge

The basic goal for monitoring knowledge is to determine how well it is producing value in corporate processes. This requires following the use of knowledge throughout an organization's core processes and its interactions with the marketplace. As an organization interacts with its customers and competitors, it can learn what works and doesn't work. It learns from its customers what products and services are valued because customers are willing to pay for them. It also learns that its competitors are not far behind. This learning must be transformed into actionable activities within core processes to develop and produce ever more appealing products and services. The rate at which this knowledge can be transformed into corporate core process knowledge will determine how quickly value is created through the offering of new products and services.

1. Accelerate the learning-knowledge-value cycle through monitoring of the transformation process.

Self-organizing systems follow a sense-monitor-and-respond approach, which differs from Industrial Age command-and-control approaches. Interfaces can be used to elicit direct comment from customers about company products and services. Running tallies of sales and customer comments can be mined to interpret responses from the marketplace.[9] These activities usually support evolutionary developments. Research and development efforts to create "truly new" products and services require more complex analysis and synthesis of market responses to company offerings.

Transforming these learnings into core process knowledge must also be monitored. Fortunately, there is software available to monitor an enterprise and how well it transforms learnings into core process performance (see, for example, Enterprise Strategist and the monitoring-learning tool suite from Intelligent Systems Technology, Inc.). These software suites allow management to determine how much value new knowledge produces when embedded in core processes.

This knowledge-monitoring principle requires corporate management to go beyond the traditional view of "build it and they will come." Management must accelerate the pace at which they embed critical marketplace learnings within their core processes. And, they must go a step further and determine what value the introduction of this new knowledge produces. If embedding does not produce good return on the new knowledge, then management has done a poor job of synthesizing learnings from the marketplace or the marketplace has changed, making the new embedded knowledge less valuable.

Conducting a knowledge-gap assessment aids management in determining the gaps in knowledge necessary for current operations. The assessment can identify knowledge assets that will be required to produce future value. Combining the concepts of sense, monitor and respond with a knowledge-gap assessment will help management identify the most promising knowledge for embedding in core processes.

2. Identify existing and future knowledge gaps.

Monitoring the learning-knowledge-value cycle will reveal gaps in current performance. Planning for future products and services will reveal gaps in knowledge required to produce these future products and services.

Corporations must draw on the "knowledge marketplace" to fill its current and future gaps. The first step is to identify these gaps in the corporate knowledge portfolio, and the knowledge-gap assessment is a powerful method for identifying the gaps.

- Begin with a definition or mapping of core processes in terms of the knowledge required to conduct normal operations.
- Make a list of the knowledge potential not currently in use within the core processes.
- Make a list of the knowledge no longer necessary to successfully generate the outputs.

[9]"Fad Tracker"™ allows companies to subscribe to a service that provides near instantaneous feedback on which new products and services are reaching critical mass and may present competition and/or new opportunities to existing firms.

- List the kinds of knowledge the company will need in the future to meet its long- and short-term goals.
- Compare the current knowledge assets deployed in the processes and identify the gaps between this and the untapped knowledge potential currently available and future knowledge required to meet new market demands.

This simple gap analysis motivates managers to recognize the untapped intellectual capital residing in their employees as well as the contributions of existing information technology. The results provide a framework for developing the requirements for upgrades or replacements.

Enhancing, maintaining, and acquiring knowledge assets to fill knowledge gaps is one of management's most significant duties. The basic steps to follow in filling and maintaining knowledge assets are:

- List the methods to maintain the current level of knowledge assets deployed.
- List the methods to remove the knowledge that is no longer needed.
- List the methods to narrow or remove the gaps in knowledge needed and knowledge assets currently available.
- List current strategies for knowledge maintenance and acquisition through hiring, training, outsourcing, information systems, and work rules.

Filling knowledge gaps and maintaining current valuable knowledge assets can involve the company's information systems, human resources, and strategy areas, as well as the specific core process owners affected. As with any portfolio decision, there are multiple interdependent outcomes. For example, embedding critical knowledge in IT in an upstream process may produce bottlenecks in downstream processes that have not been upgraded. These interdependencies can be examined with work-flow software before making final decisions requiring significant investment.

3. Identify the best practices for embedding knowledge in IT, people, and processes.

Best practices in knowledge management have been benchmarked by the American Productivity and Quality Center and at Arthur Andersen and are available in various forms from both organizations.

4. Measure the value-added by knowledge to create an internal marketplace.

This principle can be followed best by creating a simple accounting system to monitor knowledge utilization. The knowledge accounting system should allow managers to establish a price and cost per unit of knowledge. The price and cost must be tied directly to companies' normal financial performance measures such as ROI, cash flow, and earnings per share.

This principle provides management with feedback about how well they are managing the learning-knowledge-value cycle. Providing price and cost per unit of knowledge will lead to new performance ratios such as

- Knowledge in use compared to knowledge in inventory.
- Total knowledge compared to amount reused.
- Knowledge in people compared to knowledge in IT.

Such measurement systems, when adopted by the accounting community, will lead to better protections for investors in companies with large market capitalization based on intangible assets contained in intellectual capital.

CONCLUSION

This chapter reviewed a very preliminary set of knowledge management principles. The problem is not to expand this set of principles: The problem is to refine these to the most fundamental few. To move the study and practice of knowledge management to a higher plane requires a powerful framework that will lead us to a common understanding of what best represents a common "unit" of knowledge. Finding such a unit is a vital part of building a comprehensive framework for knowledge management. Once we know what it is we are "looking at," we can track it, transform it, embed it, count it, retain it, and use it to create more knowledge.

For the time being at least, we must be satisfied with a set of general principles. Even though these guidelines are less than explicit, we should not give up on this new management approach and on creating a more stable and objective level of understanding.

We may discover that the old ideal—a truth that remains binding in diverse circumstances in spite of the passage of time—is itself inadequate. Just as our search for subatomic "basic building blocks" has led us to the conundrum of observer-dependent phenomena, so our pursuit of ultimate knowledge management principles may well result in new definitions for what we mean by "ultimate" and "principles." Just as Einstein and others had to settle for the conflicting paradigms of wave, field, and particle in attempting to describe the phenomenon of light, so we may find ourselves using apparently irreconcilable descriptors to capture the complexity of human knowledge as it expresses itself in the business environment.

QUESTIONS FOR REVIEW

1. Why is knowledge management expected to have such a significant impact on business? Do you agree or disagree with the book on this issue? Why?
2. What is missing from the knowledge management initiatives to make them successful in the Internet marketplace?
3. What are some of the general guidelines for developing a knowledge management strategy?
4. What is driving the need for such a strategy?
5. How should the relationship between customer and transaction knowledge guide the development of a knowledge management strategy?
6. What are some general principles for moving knowledge into information technology?

7. How can you justify moving the knowledge to information technology?
8. What are the benefits of monitoring and measuring knowledge usage?

CASE STUDY: The Distance Learning Case

Taken together, public and private colleges and universities in the United States comprise a $200 billion industry where knowledge is for sale. Throughout the 20th century, these institutions had difficulty achieving economies of scale. The number of students served by an individual faculty member across school averaged 20-to-1 per class taught, a ratio enforced by size limitations of classrooms, faculty resistance to grading larger numbers of tests and papers, and the desire for smaller classes and individuation of learning on the part of students and parents.

To achieve competitive advantage, institutions pursued various strategies, including hiring famous faculty as an inducement for student enrollment, pouring resources into high-interest fields (e.g., computer science) and canceling low-interest programs (e.g., Latin), scheduling classes at times and places conducive to student life, farming alumni resources more assiduously, and maximizing college name recognition and reputation through nationally ranked sports teams.

Due to the pervasive tenure system, most colleges and universities do not have the option of "right-sizing" by firing expensive senior faculty to hire inexpensive junior faculty, even though this alternative would yield extraordinary savings in institutional costs per student educated. It has occurred to such schools that the only practical way to significantly increase the per student load of each faculty member (and thereby increase system productivity) was to broadcast the image, voice, and learning materials of the instructor to a broader audience.

Enter distance learning. With the combined technologies of the Internet, e-mail, and video teleconferencing, educational institutions are able to enroll exponentially more students at home or at remote sites without increasing the number of faculty members employed or their salaries. Additional grading responsibilities involved in distance learning can be delegated to graduate teaching assistants working at not much above minimum wage. Famous and popular faculty members can be given large electronic audiences, thereby maximizing their influence on behalf of the institution. Less successful teachers could be confined to traditional face-to-face instruction, thereby minimizing their impact on the reputation and welfare of the institution.

This case asks you to extrapolate the implications of distance learning for the design and workings of colleges and universities of the future. As knowledge is managed in new ways, dramatic changes may be in store for these institutions. In your speculations, consider the following:

- Physical requirements of the new "campus."
- Instructor qualifications, including preparation for distance learning.
- Viability of traditional "courses," "majors," and "degrees."
- Interactive versus "canned" instruction. (Would you prefer to learn from Professor X interactively or from Einstein via videotape?)

- The loss of unmeasurables when the traditional face-to-face classroom is superseded electronically.
- Compensation and career paths for faculty. (Will research be of less importance as a faculty member more and more plays the role of anchor person or mouthpiece in distance learning?)
- Links with or mergers with corporations. (Will/should corporate universities swallow up public and private institutions?)
- Is distance learning more appropriate for some subjects than others? For some types of students?

Attempt to draw together your speculations into a design for future knowledge management useful for present institutions of higher learning.

5

KNOWLEDGE MANAGEMENT AT WORK IN ORGANIZATIONS

For most business readers, definitions and principles are less approachable and certainly less memorable than concrete "war stories." This chapter describes the contemporary uses for knowledge management in a variety of industries as well as positive and negative results of this new management approach.

As you read, please keep the "Hawthorne effect" in mind. New approaches often appear to outstrip older methods because of the enthusiasm they generate. As a result, it is best to view especially the most enthusiastic results and responses from knowledge management initiatives as early and tentative in nature.

Moreover, new initiatives may not be portable to different industries and applications. Knowledge management, like a complex living organism, usually exists in close interdependence with its specific environment. Managing knowledge in a cardiac care unit may link only tangentially with managing knowledge in chip-manufacturing plants. Each environment determines the nature, scope, and tolerances for the knowledge at the core of its processes. What may seem lax and fuzzy in one management environment may be necessary for another. For example, the rigidity and specificity of knowledge management in a laboratory may be wholly unsuited to the management of knowledge in the boardroom.

KNOWLEDGE MANAGEMENT IN PRACTICE

Organizations around the world are adopting knowledge management practices at an accelerating pace. They have combined cultural and procedural changes with enabling technology to realize bottom-line improvements. A number of comprehensive surveys have indicated that organizations are engaged in wide-ranging efforts to implement and improve knowledge management practices. This section will highlight some of the more noteworthy initiatives and survey results.

In a recent survey of 36 vendors and 650 evaluators, the Delphi Consulting Group found that 28 percent of the companies surveyed were using some form of knowledge management, and this figure is expected to leap to 77 percent within the next two years. In fact, 85 percent of respondents saw knowledge management as an important or essential new focus in their efforts to become more innovative and responsive to turbulent market forces.[1] (See Table 5.1.)

The Delphi survey also identified some of the principal initiatives. Twenty-five percent of respondents are creating "networks of knowledge" among employees, and another 15 percent plan to launch such a scheme. Establishing new knowledge roles is another common approach, with 15 percent of respondents involved. Just under 10 percent say they have concrete plans to create new roles, and an additional 30 percent say it's something they should be doing. Launching knowledge-based products and services is employed by 15 percent, while 15 percent plan to employ this approach and nearly 20 percent more say they should.

Ernst & Young conducted a similar survey of 431 U.S. and European companies. Ninety-four percent of respondents said they believe they could leverage the knowledge in their organizations more effectively through designed management, and more than 40 percent said they had already started or completed a knowledge management project. Another 25 percent said they plan to do so in the next year.

The survey also identified five key benefits of knowledge management initiatives. Table 5.2 lists the perceived benefits. In addition, some two-thirds of the respondents expected that improved knowledge management would provide organizational benefits by reducing costs (68 percent); increasing flexibility to adapt and change (67 percent); reducing the time-to-market for new products/services (67 percent); increasing sales (65 percent); and reducing process cycle times (62 percent).

Another notable Ernst & Young finding is that most of the participants are approaching knowledge management as a series of separate, often unconnected initiatives rather than as a holistic business strategy. This approach is similar to one adopted by companies in the mid-1980s as they attempted to introduce aspects of total quality management (TQM) without addressing the key issue of developing an integrated strategic view of TQM.[2]

Although some organizations are clearly struggling to find appropriate knowledge management practices, a number of progressive companies are beginning to manage the

TABLE 5.1   TIMETABLE FOR INVESTMENTS IN KNOWLEDGE MANAGEMENT[3]

Already have it	28%
Will have it within the next year	21%
Will have it in the next 1–4 years	49%
Will never invest in it	2%

[1]"Delphi Initiates Coverage of Knowledge Management: Announces Knowledge Management Report Findings," Delphi Consulting Group, Inc. Press Release, July 23, 1997.

[2]Rory Chase, "Creating the Knowledge-Based Organization," 1997: http://benchdb.com/kmmssurvey/report.htm.

[3]"Delphi Initiates Coverage of Knowledge Management: Announces Knowledge Management Report Findings," Delphi Consulting Group, Inc. Press Release, July 23, 1997, p. 1.

TABLE 5.2   PERCEIVED BENEFITS FROM KNOWLEDGE MANAGEMENT[4]

Improved decision making	89%
Improved responsiveness to customers	84%
Improved efficiency of people and operations	82%
Improved innovation	73%
Improved products/services	73%

vast stores of knowledge within their organizations in formal, strategic manners. Companies are establishing formal knowledge management functions and assigning executives from line groups or relevant support groups to lead them. For example, General Electric has a chief learning officer; Monsanto has a vice president of Knowledge Management; and Dow Chemical has created a position for a global director of Intellectual Assets and Capital Management. A recent A. D. Little survey found that although titles vary, 42 percent of Fortune 500 companies have a chief knowledge officer.

In some cases, company CIOs are redesigning their roles to meet growing needs for knowledge management. For example, Hewlett-Packard and General Motors have CIOs who have expanded their roles beyond the mere provisioning of information technology into accepting the broader challenge of improving the way their companies manage and leverage organizational knowledge. Other companies rely on midlevel managers to accomplish the transition to knowledge management. These champions of knowledge management practice are charged with the task of proving the worth of knowledge management upward, downward, and across decentralized organizational structures. Table 5.3 lists titles at representative companies.

Firms that are actively exploring knowledge management include the World Bank, Skandia, Hewlett-Packard, Canadian Imperial Bank, Chase Manhattan, Chevron, Chaparral Steel, BP, US West, Stentor,[5] Dow Chemical, Hughes Space and Communications, and Monsanto. While the efforts of some are more formal than of others, all are exploring new ways to accelerate learning and leverage knowledge.

Dow Chemical

Four years ago Dow Chemical completed a knowledge management project to evaluate one of the company's intellectual assets—its 30,000 patents. By identifying patents that continue to contain value, Dow planned to boost licensing royalties from $20 million in 1997 to $125 million by year-end 2000. It also plans to cut $40 million in tax maintenance over 10 years by identifying unused patents that it can allow to expire.

[4]Ernst & Young Center for Business Innovation and Business Intelligence survey, 1997.
[5]Stentor is in the process of being disbanded. However, the company's experience in the knowledge management arena offers some useful insights to others in approaching the management of knowledge as a strategic direction.

TABLE 5.3   KNOWLEDGE MANAGEMENT POSITIONS

Company	Title
Arthur Andersen	Global Knowledge Manager
Booz Allen & Hamilton	Chief Knowledge Officer and Sr. VP
Bucknowledge Management and Labs	VP of Knowledge Transfer
Canadian Imperial Bank of Commerce	VP Knowledge-Based Business
Coopers & Lybrand	Vice Chairman, Chief Knowledge Officer
Dow Chemical	Intellectual Asset Management for New Business and Central Research
Dow Chemical	Intangible Asset Appraiser, Intellectual Asset Management
Dow Chemical	Global Director, Intellectual Assets and Capital Management
Ernst & Young	Chief Knowledge Officer
General Electric	Chief Learning Officer
Hewlett-Packard Company	Program Manager, Program Management Program
Hughes Space & Communications Co.	Leader, Learning and Change
IBM Consulting	Director of Knowledge Management and Asset Reuse
ICL	Program Director, Knowledge Management
KNOWLEDGE MANAGEMENT PG	Director of Knowledge Management
Monitor Company	Chief Knowledge Officer
Monsanto	VP of Knowledge Management; Director, Knowledge Management
NatWest Markets	Chief Knowledge Officer
Odwalla, Inc.	SVP, Chief Learning Officer
PeopleSoft	Manager, Knowledge Development Team
Philip Morris	Knowledge Management Champion
Skandia AFS	Director, Intellectual Capital
Texas Instruments	Office of Best Practices
US West	Internal Knowledge Management Consultant
Xerox Corporation	Director, Intellectual Asset Management

These revenues and savings have convinced top managers at Dow to make knowledge management a companywide initiative. Dow is now evaluating ways to capture workers' business processes expertise and use it throughout the international operations of the company. Dow also believes that the ability to share knowledge with companies in developing nations offers an opportunity to enter lucrative partnerships with key players in those countries. For example, Dow could offer technical know-how to a company that could in turn provide manufacturing facilities, supplies, and employees. That has convinced top executives at Dow of the bottom-line value of strategic knowledge management.

The World Bank

The World Bank is an organization owned by many of the governments of the world. It lends money to support economic development and provides advice. In 1996, the president made an announcement that forced the firm to make changes in how knowledge was managed. He announced that the organization was going to manage and share its knowledge with clients around the world via the Internet and other methods. The goal of the initiative is to make World Bank knowledge available in a database to provide assistance for all personnel.

The conceptual model they are using treats knowledge management as a process of creating, organizing, and applying data. The organization as a whole has these seven goals.

1. Assembling a large knowledge base in a knowledge management system.
2. Creating a help desk that can help users find the things they need.
3. Establishing an experts directory.
4. Developing data and statistics on changes in each country.
5. Articulating engagement information and links within the organization.
6. Providing dialog space for questions, answers, and conversations.
7. Facilitating access to users outside the organization.

At this point the World Bank is still trying to make this whole process a success and convince skeptics that an organization known for its static ways can change into an organization of the times.[6]

Skandia

In the early 1980s, managers at Skandia found that traditional management and accounting theories did not accurately reflect value found within their company. Since Skandia is a knowledge-intensive service company, its inventory was only a fraction of its assets. Reports strove to define new methods of valuation and described ways to attach importance to a company's intangible assets.

Leif Edvisson, the director of the Swedish Coalition of Service Industries, was named director of the intellectual capital management function for the AFS business unit of Skandia in 1991. This was part of the effort to capture and define the value of intellectual capital as a complement to the balance sheet. CEO Bjorn Wolrath and top executive Jan Carendi viewed intellectual capital (IC) reporting as a tool to aid internal decisions and descriptions of the company's knowledge assets to the shareholders.

Rapid growth occurred in the AFS division under Edvisson from 1991 to 1995, and he strove to create a system that could make the growth truly appreciated. During these years alliances grew from 50,000 to 65,000, and the employee count increased from 1,100 to 2,000 during the same period. In May 1995, the IC team released the first public IC annual report as a supplement to the financial report, and over 500 corporations

[6]Chris Meyer and Rudy Ruggles, *The Knowledge Advantage: Leveraging Knowledge into Marketplace Success.* (Boston: Butterworth Heinemann, 1999), p. 143–61.

have contacted Edvisson for assistance in developing their own IC reports. Skandia's effort was not the first attempt to manage knowledge, but it was the most concentrated, and by doing so publicly they set the trend for other companies to follow suit.[7]

Hewlett-Packard

At Hewlett-Packard, employees used the intranet to facilitate communication and knowledge sharing. The HP intranet consisted of 2,500 computers and sent out over 1.5 million e-mails a day. Former Chief Executive Lew Platt claimed that HP had been using an intranet since 1989, before the term even existed. All of this created a conducive environment for knowledge sharing both internally and externally. The intranet allowed collaboration within the organization to work better for the customer.

Internally, the intranet was used for product management, online conversations, and the Electronic Sales Partner. Product management through the intranet allowed for all divisions involved to collaborate and improved both product scheduling and time to market. More than 100 internal newsgroups were formed, and employees discussed a variety of topics. The Electronic Sales Partner allowed sales representatives access to over 10,000 current documents. There was also an external aspect to the intranet that allowed customers to access information and contact HP directly.[8]

Core Competencies at Chase Manhattan and Canadian Imperial Bank of Commerce

Chase Manhattan has identified their core competencies as the way to succeed in the face of increased competition and a growing international focus. Corporate core competencies in each market segment have been identified, and Chase is changing the organization of the employees of the company. Instead of having traditional jobs, Chase has begun to recognize employee competencies in people that help the customer, matching employee skills with customer needs.

The focus on individual competencies has changed recruiting, performance standards, and career development by shaping them around competency definitions. Instead of the traditional ladder of positions, levels are defined by expertise, ranging from "minimal knowledge" up to "advisory." By linking individual competencies and company competencies, employees can organize themselves into effective teams. This new focus at Chase is sustained by databases and information technology that reflect the fact that people do not fit into one position and their individual skills and knowledge are valued.

The Canadian Imperial Bank of Commerce also saw the value of a competency model. With the shift to the competency model, CIBC basically eliminated $30 million of training and related management costs. What CIBC did was describe key knowledge and skill competencies that provide value to the customer. Each employee

---

[7]Huseman and Goodman, *Leading with Knowledge,* pp. 174–76.

[8]David Skyrme, *Knowledge Networking: Creating the Collaborative Enterprise.* (Boston: Butterworth Heinemann, 1999), p. 89.

is expected to master key skills by studying books and software available in each branch's learning room.[9]

Chevron

Chevron's Information Management Services Group is transforming itself from a cost center to a profit center. Challenges include lost service requests for data and information and poor management of the contracting processes.

The Information Services Group needed to demonstrate its value by creating and distributing a "service value portfolio" that showed what services it offered. Additional requirements included a knowledge framework for categorization of its library materials and information services as well as knowledge navigators to help other employees find the information they needed.

In the process of doing all this, Chevron identified knowledge and performance gaps that led it to discover the levels of knowledge work needed for each product. The result is a more accurate reflection of product costs and more accurate contract estimates, in addition to an increase in unit cost recovery, customer response and satisfaction, internal and external value-adding partnerships, recognition for their part in knowledge creation, and development of individual and team competencies.[10]

Chaparral Steel

At Chaparral Steel, enhancing knowledge is a constant goal. According to Dorothy Leonard-Barton, author of *Wellsprings of Knowledge,* the company achieves this through three internal activities and one external activity. The three internal activities are shared creative problem solving, implementing and integrating new methodologies and tools, and formal and informal experimentation. The external activity is pulling in outside expertise.

As a result there is a culture of high sharing that has helped to remove many vertical and horizontal obstacles. Employees are not placed in one job area, and production workers are free to share their views in any problem situation. Lead operators are chosen based on their skills in sharing and creating knowledge. All of this has contributed to an innovative environment that results in constant benchmarking, externally looking for ideas, and continuous experimentation.[11]

Knowledge Networking at British Petroleum (BP)

BP has a very decentralized infrastructure that relies on information technology such as videoconferencing. There are many virtual teams that share knowledge and make independent choices. Multimedia e-mail, document management, Lotus Notes, and an

---

[9]Verna Allee, *The Knowledge Evolution: Expanding Organizational Intelligence.* (Boston: Butterworth Heinemann, 1997), pp. 28–29.
[10]Ibid., pp. 72–73.
[11]Ibid., pp. 208–9.

intranet are vital parts of the knowledge exchange. In 1994 BP deployed extensive videoconferencing to support virtual teams. By enhancing communication, it also increased trust between remote workers.

Benefits reported by BP include speedier completion of knowledge transactions by allowing dispersed members to come together, making connections across distances that normally would require expensive travel, and making these connections stronger and more extensive because of the ease of multiple transactions that can take place through videoconferencing. The more trusting relationships that form as a result of committing to someone personally results in a higher commitment than e-mail normally would. All of the success that has resulted from virtual teams is contingent on the coaches that work with these teams.[12]

Monsanto[13]

When Monsanto reorganized itself into 14 business units, the St. Louis–based chemicals company built principles of knowledge management into the new structures. Monsanto designed a system of flexible business units. These units can combine easily into functional teams focused on specific problems, exchange knowledge to solve a particular problem, and then break apart to address new issues.

Monsanto's IT group designed a knowledge-management architecture to support the new organization. The group decided the architecture had to include both structured and unstructured data from inside and outside the company. To support the structured data, the company built an enterprisewide data warehouse and standardized tools for online analytical processing. Unstructured data is stored in the form of documents in Lotus Notes databases and Documentum Inc.'s document-management system (reviewed in Chapter 8).

Monsanto also designated formal roles for people in its knowledge-management system. The company appointed topic experts to analyze and identify material to be added to the knowledge base. And, it assigned stewards to ensure that dialogue occurred between departments. "Technology plays a very vital role in knowledge management, but technology on its own cannot make knowledge management happen," says Bipin Junarkar, the company's director of knowledge management.[14]

More Current Applications

The applications described above are a fraction of current initiatives. Table 5.4 provides a more comprehensive synopsis of current initiatives.

---

[12]Skyrme, *Knowledge Networking,* p. 113.
[13]Laurie Payne, "Unlocking an Organization's Ultimate Potential Through Knowledge Management," *Knowledge Management in Practice.*
[14]Justin Hibbard, "Knowledge Management—Knowing What We Know," *Information Week,* October 27, 1997.

TABLE 5.4   KNOWLEDGE MANAGEMENT PRACTICES

Company	Country	Knowledge Management Objectives	Knowledge Management Practices and Initiatives
3M	USA	Build knowledge-sharing culture.	Managers are required to link continuous learning to revenues.
Analog Devices	USA	Build knowledge-sharing culture.	CEO Ray Stata initiated breakdown of functional barriers and competitive atmosphere and created a collaborative knowledge-sharing culture from the top. Company encourages "community of inquirers" rather than "community of advocates."
Boeing 777	USA	Build knowledge-sharing culture.	First "paperless" development of aircraft. Included customers in design teams. More than 200 teams with wide range of skills both designed and constructed subparts, rather than usual organization design team and construction team. Suppliers worldwide used same digital databases as Boeing.
Buckman Labs	USA	1. Build knowledge-sharing culture. 2. Create careers based on knowledge management.	A biotech firm that has reorganized itself to optimize knowledge sharing. Created a Knowledge Transfer Department to coordinate efforts. Employees best at knowledge sharing gain both financial rewards and management positions.
Chaparral Steel	USA	Build knowledge-sharing culture.	Mini steel mill that has introduced broad range of initiatives such as: flat hierarchy, broad education, blue-collar workers responsible for customer contacts and rewarded for personal initiatives. Chaparral uses 1.5 hrs. labor per ton; industry standard of 1.5–3.0 hrs. per ton.
Ford Motor	USA	Build knowledge-sharing culture.	Company that has transformed itself by outsourcing and creating virtual networks of vendors using IT.
Oticon	Denmark	Build knowledge-sharing culture.	Has created a "spaghetti organization," a chaotic tangle of interrelationships and interactions. Knowledge workers have no fixed job descriptions but work entirely on project basis.
Hewlett-Packard	USA	1. Build knowledge-sharing culture. 2. Create micro-environments for tacit knowledge transfer.	Implemented an overall culture of collaboration, which encourages knowledge sharing and risk taking on all levels. H-P even supports people who try out things that don't work.
Affaers-vaerlden	Sweden	Create micro-environments for tacit knowledge transfer.	Business journal uses "piggy-backing" and "team-writing" to speed up learning among new journalists. Interviews and larger articles are routinely assigned as team work, rather than one-man shows. This speeds up transfer of the seniors' tacit skills and networks to the juniors.

(continued)

TABLE 5.4 KNOWLEDGE MANAGEMENT PRACTICES *(continued)*

Company	Country	Knowledge Management Objectives	Knowledge Management Practices and Initiatives
Honda	Japan	Create micro-environments for tacit knowledge transfer.	"Redundancy" routinely used; people are given information that goes beyond their immediate operational requirements. This facilitates sharing in responsibilities and creative solutions from unexpected sources and acts as a self-control mechanism.
PLS-Consult	Denmark	1. Measure knowledge-creating processes and intangible assets. 2. Create micro-environments for tacit knowledge transfer.	Categorizes customers according to value of knowledge contribution to the firm. Follows up in management information system. Appoints "mentors" with task to facilitate transfer of tacit skills between members in large projects. Actively seeks large projects, so that junior consultants can be added to the teams for learning.
Agro	USA	Offer customers additional knowledge.	Data on farmers and soils are combined with weather forecasts and information on crops. Analyses are fed back to the farmer via sales reps to help farmer select best combinations of crops.
Frito-Lay	USA	Offer customers additional knowledge.	Sales reps collect daily spot data about shelf space utilization for all brands. Data are computed, combined with market information, and refed to the sales reps, who use it to give the retailers information on best shelf utilization.
Benetton	Italy	Gain customer knowledge.	Produces "mass-customized" apparel to fit latest trends in colors and designs. Daily sales data from their own boutiques are integrated with computer-aided design and computer-integrated manufacturing.
General Electric	USA	Gain customer knowledge.	Since 1982, the company has collected all customer complaints in a database that supports telephone operators in answering customer calls. GE has programmed 1.5 million potential problems and their solutions into its system.
National Bicycle	Japan	Gain customer knowledge.	Produces "mass-customized" bikes to fit customers' exact height, weight, and color preferences in a day. Is achieved through computer-aided design and computer-integrated manufacturing integrated with customer database.
Netscape	USA	Gain customer knowledge.	Very close links via Internet to opinion leaders among customers, who are encouraged to report problems to enable it to create new generations of software at a very fast pace.

TABLE 5.4   KNOWLEDGE MANAGEMENT PRACTICES *(concluded)*

Company	Country	Knowledge Management Objectives	Knowledge Management Practices and Initiatives
Ritz Carlton	Worldwide	Gain customer knowledge.	Staff required to fill out cards with information from every personal encounter with a guest. Data plus all guest requirements are stored and printed out to all staff when the guest arrives again, so that each guest receives personal treatment.
British Petroleum	UK	Capture, store, and spread individuals' tacit knowledge.	Using knowledge management to draw together talents from all over the organization. BP emphasizes transfer of tacit knowledge rather than accumulation and transmission of raw data and has installed a communication network comprising videoconferencing, multimedia, and e-mail.
Chevron	USA	Capture, store, and spread individuals' tacit knowledge.	Created a "best practice" database that captures experience of drilling conditions and innovative solutions to problems on site in a database for sharing globally with other sites.
McKinsey and Bain & Co.	USA	Capture, store, and spread individuals' tacit knowledge.	These two management consulting firms have developed "knowledge databases" that contain experiences from every assignment including names of team members and client reactions. Each team must appoint a "historian" to document the work.
Dow Chemical	USA	Create new revenues from existing knowledge.	Puts all its 25,000+ patents into a database, which is used by all divisions to explore how existing patents can gain more revenues. The experience from this application is now being transferred into other intellectual assets.
Outoku-mppu	Finland	Create new revenues from existing knowledge.	Knowledge on how to build smelting plants is used to construct whole plants including education of personnel and managers to customers all over the world. This business is now more profitable than its original business base.
Steelcase	USA	Create new revenues from existing knowledge.	Does basic research into innovation and learning, best learning environments, and new interfaces (3D and virtual tools). Steelcase sells its knowledge in this area to other companies.
IBM	USA	Create careers based on knowledge management.	Employees are encouraged to switch between professional and managerial jobs in order to gain more holistic knowledge about the company.
Celemi	Sweden	Measure knowledge-creating processes and intangible assets.	Published first audit of its intangible assets in Annual Report 1995.
Telia	Sweden	Measure knowledge-creating processes and intangible assets.	Sweden's Telecom company publishes since 1990 an annual Statement of Human Resources including a profit and loss account visualizing human resource costs and a balance sheet showing investments in human resources.

Source: Karl Sveiby, "What Is Knowledge Management?" website (as of October 2000), http://www.sveiby.com.au/KnowledgeManagement.html.

It is interesting to note the large number of Swedish companies involved in knowledge management. Swedish companies have been pioneers in this field and were the first to monitor and systemize intelligence activities in large European companies. Observations at Astra-Draco, Ericsson Radio, Gambro, Celsius Tech, Skandia, SAS, Telia, and Volvo identified four common features:[15]

1. Balance between strategy and operational objectives.
2. A systematic supply-on-demand intelligence for corporate management.
3. A focus on information-sharing cultures, including systematic community meetings linking businesspeople, academics, and military officers.
4. Emphasis on knowledge-sharing acquisition processes.

According to Professor Philippe Baumard at the University of Paris, several reasons account for Swedish supremacy in this arena. First, information sharing is a long-standing cultural practice among the Swedes. Second, the core of the Swedish knowledge infrastructure is a "community of practice and sense-making rather than a hardware-based infrastructure."[16] In addition, Professor Baumard observes that one of the first business intelligence courses was started in Sweden by Dr. Steven Dedijer. In 1997, he launched a business intelligence course at Lund University in Sweden, and many graduate students subsequently became the managers directing economic intelligence groups in Skandia, Volvo, and Ericsson.[17]

CONCLUSION

It is clear from this review that knowledge management practices are increasing at a nearly exponential rate. In many cases, the process begins with demonstration projects or more limited initiatives that prove the value of the new approach. The evidence supports a typical S-shaped adoption curve paralleling marketing and biological phenomena. For example, epidemics spread from linear periods to exponential spreads that affect large groups.

The actual practices employed by knowledge management professionals come from a wide range of industries and companies. As a result, they provide helpful hints and models that can be applied across industries. Information technology is driving many practices, but the technology alone does not ensure success. Some of the keys appear to be:

- An emphasis on a clearly defined goal for such knowledge management practice.
- Allowing experimentation among the initiators.
- Using technology to capture, store, and distribute knowledge.
- Finding new ways to obtain and share knowledge with customers.
- Reusing valuable knowledge as often as possible.
- Making sure that the impact of practices can be tracked to the bottom line.

[15]Philippe Baumard, "From InfoWar to Knowledge Warfare: Preparing for the Paradigm Shift," Intelligence Online, 1997: http://www.indigo-net.com/annexes/289/.
[16]Ibid, p. 36.
[17]Ibid.

Such key learnings are a good beginning for successful knowledge management practices. Initiators of knowledge management practices must keep one eye on corporate strategy and one eye on practical implementation within core processes. The company cases included in this chapter offer some examples of how knowledge management practices can make a difference to corporate bottom lines and core processes and become a central theme in management strategies.

QUESTIONS FOR REVIEW

1. What impact will potential investment in knowledge management practices have on job creation in the field?
2. What kinds of jobs, at all levels, are most likely to be created?
3. What is the best way to position yourself for one of these jobs?
4. What are some of the general principles for successful knowledge management that can be derived from the case examples?
5. When is it best to start a knowledge management effort from the top? From the bottom?
6. What kinds of concrete benefits were demonstrated from the knowledge management practices and initiatives?
7. When and how will the United States catch up with the Scandinavian countries in knowledge management practices?

CASE STUDY: The United Radiology Case

Internists, orthopedists, urologists, and others view and interpret their patients' X rays, CAT scans, and MRI results. Previously, these physicians relied upon trained radiologists to read such films and report on their findings. Under this arrangement, radiologists would charge both for physical administration of the test at hand and for its analysis.

As doctors have reclaimed the analysis function, large radiology corporations such as United Radiologists, with 12,000 employees in 34 states, saw revenues erode throughout the late 1990s even as the total numbers of examined patients increased. In early 1999, the corporation's executive committee convened a large panel of its radiologists to work with William Forest, Ph.D., a noted business consultant for medical companies.

Forest began the daylong session by reviewing United Radiology's hard numbers—decreasing gross revenues and profits. He pointed out that the trend line was moving steeply downward at an ever-increasing rate, and the viability of the company would be threatened within two years.

Stunned by the gravity of the situation, panel members asked Forest, "What can we do?" The following conversation ensued:

Forest: Tell me what you do.
Panel member: We administer a variety of radiology tests and interpret the results.
Forest: So you are in the testing business?

Panel members: Yes.

Forest: I disagree. I think you are in the knowledge business.

Panel member: What do you mean?

Forest went on to explain that radiologists made money by selling their expertise for a price. United Radiology, he concluded, was losing its profitability because it lost its focus on its core business: the sale of knowledge. In effect, Forest said, other doctors were saying "I can do that!" and grabbing the business that formerly belonged exclusively to radiologists. These doctors no longer felt that the knowledge imparted by radiologists was different in kind or quality from the knowledge they themselves could bring to the reading of X-ray films and other test results.

According to Forest, the business solution for United Radiology's economic woes did not lie in trying to process more and more patients per hour or in marketing their services to a wider group of physicians. Instead, the business solution lay in shrewd knowledge management.

Speculate how United Radiologists can reverse its downward trend by focusing on the sale of knowledge. The company has the options of making such knowledge (1) cheaper, (2) faster, and (3) better for the patient and for the physician serving the patient. For each of these categories (cheaper, faster, better), consider specific ways in which United Radiology can again achieve competitive advantage in its market. Extend your analysis to other major providers of knowledge for a price such as network and cable news services and telephone directory services.

6

KNOWLEDGE
MEASUREMENT
AND VALUE

What we measure most easily is not necessarily what we most need to measure. Take dollars, for example. Traditional accounting techniques have found it easy to count dollars, as if that calculation alone proved valuable as a predictor of company fortunes. The hue and cry have gone out that the existing accounting measures will not fill the bill for the new knowledge economy.[1] But before we dismiss traditional accounting, we must acknowledge the pragmatic reasons for its longevity.

Traditional accounting and financial measures have endured centuries of use and change because they offer a common set of terms and units of measurement that signify commonly held, universally accepted meanings regarding the entity life cycle and activities. Investors look at the comparative aggregate financial performance of companies to discern the "best bets" for investing. Corporate management uses the same raw accounting data to gauge the organization's cost performance internally, as well as against external benchmarks. Consumers buy products or services, in essence, after comparing the market-derived prices of these outputs of corporate investment in core processes. Regulators develop, implement, and enforce regulations by poring over corporate financial data.

However, traditional accounting and financial data are no longer enough. Performance is increasingly influenced by the knowledge assets held, built, and leveraged by companies. Investors, management, customers, and regulators have a need for knowledge metrics that are reliable and acceptable to the certifying bodies that have traditionally supplied financial data.

This chapter will explore the needs of various parties for such knowledge metrics. It will also briefly review traditional approaches to valuing organizational performance in order to determine the criteria knowledge metrics must meet to be acceptable to and useful for traditional business practice, certifying bodies, and new economy businesses.

---

[1]Numerous articles in academic and popular business journals have made the case against existing accounting practices (see the *Forbes ASAP* devoted to this issue—April 7, 1997). Perhaps the most compelling arguments have been made by accountants themselves (see R. K. Elliot's article in *Accounting Horizons,* 1992, "The Third Wave [Information Age] Breaks on the Shores of [Second Wave-Industrial Age] Accounting."

EXPONENTIAL GROWTH PHASE OF THE KNOWLEDGE ECONOMY

The knowledge-based economies of the United States, Europe, and Scandinavia may have finally passed through the linear growth phase of the Information Age and may be embarking on the exponential growth phase represented by the S-shaped adoption rate curve used to predict epidemics in medicine, "killer applications" in information technology, and winning products in goods-producing industries. Economists are referring to this model to explain the unusually long economic expansion in the United States (in spite of recent downturns) and the increasing productivity of knowledge-based economies.

Driving this phase is the exponential increase in the use of information technology. The article "Has the U.S. Economy Entered a Golden Era?" states, "Computer technology has revolutionized the way private industry manages the flow of products and materials. Disruptive pile-ups of unused goods and bottlenecks caused by shortages—historically major causes of economic instability—appear to be less of a threat these days. . . The Internet meanwhile is matching up sellers who once would have been saddled with excess inventories and buyers who would have searched unsuccessfully for those same goods."[2] Alan Greenspan, chair of the Federal Reserve Board, remarked, "Important technological changes have been emerging in recent years that are altering, in ways with few precedents, the manner in which we organize production, trade across countries and deliver value to consumers."[3]

By tying hundreds of millions of computers together into a common network, the Internet has turbocharged the nation's economy and is helping to generate long-elusive improvements in productivity, a critical factor in the country's ability to improve living standards.

A close look at how companies are using the Internet to save billions of dollars in distribution and transaction costs reveals a global productivity revolution in the making. From online self-service systems for employees and customers to direct sales to remote management of far-flung facilities, corporations are changing the way business gets done.

Computers themselves have been omnipresent for decades, without much measurable impact on the efficiency of the overall economy. But only in the last few years has the Internet been put to widespread commercial use, and the nation's long-stagnant productivity began to surge at about the same time, particularly in the service economy.

Government statistics aren't precise enough to show a direct relationship, but a growing number of economists note that the economy's 99-month expansion and the improved output per worker have closely paralleled the rise of the World Wide Web. They suggest the improved efficiency in the nation's manufacturing and service sectors is largely the result of Internet-based activities such as e-mail and online commerce.[4]

[2]Jonathan Peterson, "Has the U.S. Economy Entered a Golden Era?" *LA Times,* Business Section, June 27, 1999.

[3]Remarks to Congress in presenting his periodic report in June 1999.

[4]Leslie Helm, "Analysts Cite Internet's Effect on Jump in Productivity," *LA Times,* June 30, 1999.

THREATS TO EXPONENTIAL GROWTH AND HOW KNOWLEDGE METRICS WILL HELP

First

If organizations invest in information technology without regard to its impact on knowledge utilization as a tool to generate both value and revenues, exponential future growth may be halted. Yet knowledge utilization cannot be adequately captured by either traditional accounting or finance approaches to quantification. "When a company is early in its life cycle and the industry it's in is by its very nature dynamic and complex such as E-business, the company and its investors may find very little use for standard performance measures such as those based on standard accounting data. Accounting categories developed over time for established industries may not be representative of the actual structure of the firm."[5]

Accounting and finance provide a necessary structure by which to describe business activity, but when industry structures are emerging or migrating into new forms and also changing rapidly, standard accounting and finance approaches have few means of capturing these dynamics. For example, the more e-business differs from conventional business, the less useful traditional accounting may become and the more chance it will generate misleading results. Knowledge metrics, constructed from real, quantifiable data and interoperable with traditional accounting and finance approaches, will provide a much-needed segue from the old economy into the new.

Second

The slash-and-burn tactics of cost cutting that appeared to work so well in the Industrial and Information Ages were based on a diminishing returns model that no longer applies to heavily knowledge-based, intangible-asset-laden companies.[6] The primary generators of cost—employees—also happen to be the primary generators of value. Downsizing employees without regard to the value their knowledge creates is risky at best and, at worst, may represent management malfeasance. An acceptable knowledge metric that can identify the value of employee knowledge to the bottom line is one way to help management avoid "flying blindly" in the Information Age.

Third

Without knowledge metrics, knowledge will be hoarded by organizations as a scarce resource. Yet the value-producing capabilities of knowledge only enter into an exponential growth curve when knowledge is shared among all the parties involved in the value-producing process.[7]

[5]Quote from author's discussion on August 24, 2000, with Dr. C. Slaughter-Langdon on the problems of using existing accounting practices for tracking the performance of electronic businesses.

[6]Brian Arthur, "Increasing Returns versus Diminishing Returns," *Harvard Business Review,* 1997.

[7]See Verna Allee, *The Knowledge Evolution* (1997), and recent articles for a more in-depth discussion of this concept.

The Bottom Line

Knowledge metrics must be based on quantifiable, real-world-based raw data that can be rigorously and adequately captured in a common unit of measurement. In this way, they may be used to track and manage the direct impact of knowledge assets on value production. Just as methodical scientific investigation proceeds from a base of common units of measure, a knowledge "accounting" methodology must be built on new sources of raw "knowledge" data in order to be rigorous and reliable. The rigor and reliability of a commonly accepted set of knowledge metrics would prevent knowledge hoarding and prepare the way for continued exponential growth.

The impact of knowledge management depends largely on who you ask. Consumers only care about the service or product they purchase (including after-sales service, maintenance, etc.). Investors care primarily about improving their return on investment. Managers care most about making their companies run more smoothly, growing the bottom line, and satisfying customers and investors, while staying in the good graces of the regulators. Regulators are most concerned that products and services uphold laws, benefit consumers, and perform as advertised.

With these multiple perspectives, is it possible to develop knowledge metrics that satisfy the stated concerns of all parties? To provide an answer, we will examine such issues as the redefinition of service/product, the measurement of returns on knowledge at any level, and how such metrics would fit into the traditional valuation methods in use today.

THE CONSUMER AND KNOWLEDGE METRICS: REDEFINING THE PRODUCT/SERVICE

A product/service is the sum of the knowledge required to produce it. For example, if a company had a universal computer that used a universal computer language to automate all of its processes, then the computer code would represent the total amount of thermodynamic change taking place within the company as it converts inputs into outputs.

This code also would be a surrogate for all the company's outputs including its products/services. If the code could be decomposed into its "bits,"[8] then each bit would represent a virtual universal unit of the product.[9] As such, it would be possible to allocate the price per bit and cost per bit.

This kind of quantification of knowledge might lead to new pricing heuristics for products and services. As customers ask for more customization, each feature or function could be "priced" based on a common unit of product by virtue of its knowledge "bit" representation. Companies might begin to price differentiate on the amount of knowledge bits contained in their products and might eventually choose to replace existing price schemes with this knowledge-based one.

Since quantified knowledge inputs are now a surrogate for product capability, increasing the amount of knowledge inputs should increase product capabilities. If customers

---

[8]See C. Shannon, *Information Theory,* concerning the bit.

[9]See Kanevsky and Housel, *Value-Based Reengineering: A Complexity Theory Approach* (1995), INFORS, for a more complete explanation of this reasoning.

began comparison shopping for products on the basis of price per unit of knowledge, then labeling products in terms of the amount of knowledge they represent might begin to influence customer selection more than traditional features/functions. In this way, knowledge metrics become a central element of consumer trust and the branding process.

For example, two companies go into the manufacture of hang-gliders. One is a bicycle company and the other is Boeing Aircraft. A consumer would assume that Boeing's hang-glider had more knowledge bits than the bicycle company's product. Boeing's brand name would be a surrogate for the knowledge the company had accumulated as an aircraft manufacturer over the years.

Ultimately the market will be the arbiter of any pricing scheme. Companies marketing products with the claim of more knowledge bits than their competitors will not be guaranteed better customer satisfaction or higher sales revenues. But providing a new basis for price comparisons may prove very useful for customers of knowledge-intensive industries where features and functions are not always transparent and comparison shopping is difficult.

THE INVESTOR AND KNOWLEDGE METRICS: MEASUREMENT OF RETURNS AT ALL LEVELS

For knowledge management to be taken seriously, investors must be able to determine how it benefits their ROI. Investors typically work at the level of the entity and focus on analyzing company financial performance. They rarely go below the surface to see how an organization actually produces value. This is largely because they have never had satisfactory instruments to analyze the internal workings of a firm without becoming an expert in a given industry or company.

This ignorance of a firm's value drivers becomes problematic as investors look at early-stage companies in areas such as electronic commerce or biotechnology. Such companies generally have no track record, few tangible assets, and, often, very young and inexperienced management teams. Such companies also often report negative earnings per share and yet they still find investors. Investors are betting "on-the-come," on the future earnings potential of these companies without the raw data and quantifiable benchmarks to undergird their decisions.

In absence of such new metrics, investors are likely to resort to the tried and true models with which they are familiar from the Industrial Era: namely, those based on tangible asset valuations.[10] While investors may find comfort in such methods, they are also likely to miss opportunities to select companies that are best positioned to leverage their intangible knowledge assets to produce exponential future value.

In the new economy, investors need an objective measure for evaluating early-stage companies' abilities to turn knowledge into value. Financial analysts need new tools to measure company core process performances in direct relation with their outputs. Using knowledge metrics, not only could they benchmark corporate performance

---

[10]Anomalies arise out of the existing paradigm's "Industrial Age—Mechanics" inability to explain and predict the behavior of such companies in the investment marketplace.

across industry segments, but they also would have precise, quantifiable leading indicators of how well a company is using its knowledge assets to produce value. Knowledge metrics could provide an early warning system for companies with core processes performing below benchmarked expectations, providing both the analyst and the investors they represent with tools to improve decision-making strategies.

In addition, knowledge metrics would allow the investor/analyst to drill down to any level of corporate performance necessary to become fully informed about company prospects. At the highest level of aggregation, analysts, and the investors they represent, need to know the price the market is willing to pay for a unit of knowledge as well as the cost to use a unit of knowledge in the value-generation processes of a company.

MANAGEMENT AND KNOWLEDGE METRICS: TRANSFORMING KNOWLEDGE INTO VALUE

To remain competitive, an organization's core processes must produce a bottom-line profitability that will attract investors, maintain the organization's market capitalization, and enhance corporate value production while ensuring that customers get the value they want in the products and services they receive.

Managers must constantly analyze and design processes that meet these requirements. In organizations whose growth and viability increasingly depend on rigorous deployment of knowledge assets, management needs measures that quantify the performance of core process knowledge assets and tie them directly to the bottom line. Currently, management design options are based on heuristics, "rules-of-thumb" that provide semi-empirical support for their creative strategies. However, these heuristics cannot produce codifiable insights as to whether actual or proposed changes to core processes have had or will have the desired impact on the firm's bottom line.

The use of creative knowledge represents a special case for knowledge measurement. Creative knowledge is by definition not codifiable. Trying to manage and measure this type of knowledge is problematic. For example, the value of the creative knowledge used in the research and development area of a company can only be determined after the outputs of this knowledge have been translated into core processes that produce final products. Knowledge metrics become useful for managers of creative knowledge because, using knowledge metrics, they can track the speed with which this kind of knowledge results in changes in core processes and the amount of new or changed "codifiable" knowledge in core processes. In this manner, knowledge metrics also will reveal the embedding of such creative knowledge in the company's other core processes. This provides a means to identify, quantify, and help manage the transformation of knowledge into value.

TRADITIONAL VALUATION METHODOLOGIES VIS-À-VIS KNOWLEDGE METRICS

It is critical for the successful and widespread use of knowledge metrics that they be interoperable with traditional accounting and finance valuation approaches whenever possible. Just as the theory of relativity drove physics into the next millennium, so knowledge metrics will be the driver of accounting and finance valuation methodologies.

Table 6.1 provides a brief summary of traditional valuation methodologies vis-à-vis knowledge metrics.[11]

COST, INCOME, MARKET, AND REAL OPTIONS APPROACHES

The cost, income, and market approaches are the three fundamental approaches used by the business valuation profession to value specified ownership interests in privately held companies. The real options approach was developed to value stock options but also can be applied to the problem of valuing intangible assets. The knowledge-value-added (KVA) approach will be covered in depth in Chapter 7. A review of these approaches will prove useful in framing a discussion of the general principles and practices of valuing assets, including intangibles such as knowledge.

The cost approach is based on the concept that a company is worth the market value of all its assets minus the market value of all its liabilities. For this reason, not only each balance sheet asset/liability but also each off-balance-sheet asset/liability (tangible and intangible) is identified, valued, and included on the balance sheet. Bringing the historical cost of each and every asset and liability to its current market value is time-consuming and difficult and may involve the use of additional experts to value specific categories of assets (i.e., real estate or machinery and equipment).

Variations of the cost approach are generally used to value holding and investment companies and asset-intensive companies such as those in natural resources and utilities. Asset-based methods are also reliable in early-stage companies where book values can be used as a reasonable proxy for fair market value. A particular form of the cost approach, the excess earnings approach, is regularly used to value professional practices and service companies.

The income approach is based on the concept that a company is worth the present value of its future earning power. Future economic income is projected out from the valuation date using historical trends and management's professional judgment as to the future growth of the company. If the recent history of the company's cash flows is stable and its future growth is incremental and sustainable, a single projection will be made into perpetuity. If the recent history of the company's cash flows has peaks and valleys and/or its future will involve high or uneven rates of growth, projections will be made for each year of five years (one business cycle), and then a single projection will be made from the fifth year out into perpetuity. Either way, the projected cash flows will be converted back to present value using a total rate of return on investment that is comparable to the rate of return available in the market on investments of similar risk and other characteristics. The resulting estimate of value is adjusted for whether a controlling or minority ownership interest is being valued and for the marketability or lack

---

[11]Those interested in a more thorough review of traditional valuation methodologies are directed to Pratt, Reilly, and Schweihs's book, *Valuing a Business: The Analysis and Appraisal of Closely Held Companies,* 4th ed. (New York: McGraw-Hill, 2000).

TABLE 6.1   MEASUREMENT/VALUATION METHODOLOGIES

	Cost approach	Income approach	Market approach	Real options	Knowledge value added
What is being measured/ valued?	Enterprise value and/or percent of enterprise value	Enterprise value and/or percent of enterprise value or project value	Enterprise value and/or percent of enterprise value	Project value	Contribution of knowledge to enterprise value
What valuation principle is being applied?	Enterprise value = Current cost (i.e., market value) of net tangible and identifiable intangible assets, where unidentifiable intangibles are rolled into market values of other net assets	Enterprise value = Present value of future economic income of the enterprise, as projected from historical performance	Enterprise value = Values of "guideline" publicly held companies as captured in their market multiples applied to adjusted private company data to develop private company multiples	Value of a project = Value of an option = Time (Flexibility) value + Intrinsic value	Contribution of knowledge = Value created in the change process between input and output = Revenue per knowledge unit
What is the value indicator?	Fair market value of assets and liabilities taken individually or aggregated into classes	Present value of free cash flows of subject company	P/E ratio, price/ book ratio, price/ cash flow ratio, or other relevant multiple	Net Present Value of the project	ROK, ROP
What are the data sources used?	Historical accounting data and current market cost	Historical accounting data; projected accounting data; current market rates of return on equity and debt	Historical "guideline" company data including performance ratios and market multiples; historical private company data	Market value of the stock; exercise price; free interest rate; time to maturity; volatility and amount of dividends paid	Operating/process information; historical accounting data
Unit	Dollars	Dollars	Dollars	Dollars	Dollars
How is value measured?	From current market values of assets and liabilities	From projection of future income streams based on past performance	From public market data that are reasonably comparable to subject company data	From project's immediate return + projected value to be generated in multiple outcomes	From current process analysis and close-to-current revenue data
How are intangible assets treated?	Intangibles are measured only when identifiable through placement on balance sheet or when linked to identifiable revenue streams	Intangibles are aggregated with all other assets in enterprise and enterprise/project is assessed for its ability to generate future economic income	Intangibles are aggregated with all other assets in both subject and guideline companies; become an invisible piece of "value" represented by market multiples	Intangibles not addressed directly	Knowledge, a critical intangible asset, is subject of valuation methodology
How is concept of change incorporated into methodology?	It is incorporated in a very rudimentary way by bringing historical book values up to current market value	It is tacitly incorporated into the projected economic income and into the growth rates used in cost of capital calculations	It is not incorporated	The values of flexibility and uncertainty are quantified	It is central to KVA since knowledge metrics are based on quantification of the change from input to output

(continued)

TABLE 6.1   MEASUREMENT/VALUATION METHODOLOGIES *(concluded)*

	Cost approach	Income approach	Market approach	Real options	Knowledge value added
What are the management implications of the methodologies?	Not used as a management tool	At the project level only, accept the project if NPV > 0; decision is made before the project begins; otherwise, not a management tool	Not a management tool	Allows management to identify and assess project value prior to any critical junctures during project development so optimal decisions can be made along project path	Allows management to gain critical insight into value creation of the existing processes in order to make optimal strategic decisions
How does the methodology capture and value uncertainty/risk?	Assumes uncertainty/risk captured in market data	Adjusts cash flows for uncertainty/risk; builds up discount rates by including factors for uncertainty/risk	Assumes uncertainty/risk captured in market data; adjusts market ratios for additional risk factor	Disaggregates uncertainty/risk from historical financial performance and quantifies, using option theory	Assumed to be included in revenue and cost data
Can methodologies be used across national boundaries?	Dependent on legal, regulatory, accounting, and reporting standards of each country; therefore, needs adjustments for use across national boundaries	Dependent on legal, regulatory, accounting, and reporting standards of each country; therefore, needs adjustments for use across national boundaries	Dependent on legal, regulatory, accounting, and reporting standards of each country; therefore, needs adjustments for use across national boundaries	Relatively independent of national, legal, regulatory, accounting, and reporting standards since use is internal; may need adjustment since uses options portfolios from U.S. markets	Independent of national, legal, regulatory, accounting, and reporting standards since use is internal and unit of measure is universal, not particular

of marketability of that ownership interest. The income approach is generally used to value operating companies and/or specific projects that are being proposed by management within an operating company.

The market approach is based on the concept that the value of a privately held company can be reasonably estimated by examining, adjusting, and using the market multiples (such as the price/earnings ratios) of "guideline" publicly held companies that bear enough similarity to the "subject" privately held company to make their multiples relevant.

First, the fundamental financial variables of both the subject company and its guideline companies are adjusted to make them more comparable to each other and enable the valuation professional to better assess their relative strengths and weaknesses. Financial ratios for the subject and guideline companies are calculated and compared. One or several guideline company market multiples are selected and adjusted to reflect the relative growth prospects and risks (strengths and weaknesses) of the subject company. Finally, these adjusted multiples are weighted by degree of importance and applied to the fundamental financial variables of the subject company. The resulting estimate of value is adjusted for whether a controlling or minority ownership interest is being valued and for the marketability or lack of marketability of that ownership interest. Variations of the market approach are used in conjunction with the cost and/or income approaches for valuing all kinds of companies.

The real options approach has grown out of options theory. The value of an option increases as the variability in the value of the underlying asset (cash flow per unit) increases. There are six key parameters that affect the value of a real option: the market value of the asset, the exercise price of the option, the time remaining until the option matures, the volatility of the underlying asset, the risk-free rate of the asset, and the amount of dividends paid by the underlying risky asset. This measure not only values a project's immediate return but allows inclusion of the potential value generated in multiple investment outcomes. The real options approach is a basic capital budgeting technique that focuses on measuring the value of an individual project, in conditions of uncertainty, before the project begins.

The real options approach is not used to value specified ownership interests in privately held companies but to value internal and external investment opportunities for an individual company, public or private. As such, it is a strategic business valuation tool. It is widely used by the Internet venture capital community for determining the potential future value of companies with no economic history. It also has been applied to the valuation of patents and licenses, for example, in the company PLX.com, which developed an online exchange for patents and licenses.

CONCLUSION

While it is certain that new metrics are needed to meet the requirements of all parties, it is also imperative that such metrics be endorsed and adopted by the traditional fields that generate the numbers everyone uses: accounting and finance. One approach is to try to tweak existing numbers, making the argument that these numbers provide everything already. These approaches are characterized by the "process of elimination" methods reviewed in Chapter 3. Such approaches are targeted primarily at the investor and operate at the aggregate level.

Accounting fundamentally operates at a more detailed level in generating the raw numbers that financial experts use to judge the performance of companies and industries. Any new methodology will have to posit a new raw unit of measure to reflect the leverage provided by the Information Age. To use a physics analogy, you simply would not look for a "black hole" with Newtonian physics, but such a phenomenon would be a natural outcome based on Einsteinian physics. Some might argue that the Internet marketspace is a bottomless pit within which investors pour their money; however, with the right new metrics, investors, managers, and even customers may find the real value of this new age.

Also worth noting is the cumulative effect of knowledge measurement efforts in widely differing industries and business sectors. As this body of measurement data grows, we are in an increasingly better position to recognize what measurement tools apply successfully to virtually any business and which are best limited to specific business circumstances and applications. The data also help us define and begin to deal with the large, uncharted areas of business knowledge that do not fit well within current paradigms and measurement tools.

These continuing attempts to quantify, measure, and describe knowledge in human organizations require researchers with a high tolerance for ambiguity. For now, results are more often suggestive rather than definitive. In fact, a knowledge management tool that seemed to produce definitive results across industries would for that very reason be suspect by the knowledge management community.

QUESTIONS FOR REVIEW

1. How do you think novice investors and professional investors use knowledge asset utilization in their decision-making processes?
2. How should they be using this information?
3. Where would they find such information about knowledge assets?
4. What are the inherent and practical limitations of the six approaches in valuing companies' knowledge assets?
5. How should managers use valuations of knowledge assets to guide their knowledge management decision making?
6. What will be required by the accounting and finance communities to make a knowledge valuation method acceptable?
7. Which of the six approaches is most likely to succeed in the future? Why?

CASE STUDY: Decisions at McKesson

As the largest pharmaceutical distributor in the United States with an estimated market share of 23 percent, McKesson is nevertheless struggling with relatively low profit margins, currently at only 2 percent. In endeavoring to be the right-place, right-price, right-time distributor to hospitals, doctors, drugstore chains, and small private pharmacies, McKesson faces the danger of becoming, in effect, a public service provider rather than an increasingly profitable enterprise. Increasing market share has not guaranteed profitability.

To address this problem, you and two other McKesson heavyweights have been assigned by the CEO to a Phase I Task Force to consider possible directions for re-engineering of core business processes. You are charged, first, with thinking deeply and creatively about the nature of McKesson's profit problems. At a later stage you will have corporate carte blanche to assemble a larger task force and access data as necessary to make recommendations for change.

Analyzing Business Processes
Your initial work focuses on the beating heart of McKesson's operations—its mammoth distribution center located in Santa Fe Springs, California. This facility handles the vast majority of orders, receiving and stocking tasks, and customer service requests

for the company. To date, the core processes of the distribution facility are comprised of three functions.

Standard orders, accounting for 95 percent of total orders, are stocked based on an averaging of past demand. McKesson's National Buying Center generates purchase orders for these products. The company's Electronic Data Interchange evaluates product levels every 10 days to prevent under- and overstocking of goods. Orders can be placed and filled using the electronic data interchange with only minimal human involvement.

Hand write orders account for only 2 to 3 percent of total orders, but these emergency orders (usually filled within three days) are vastly important to McKesson's customer relations. Hospitals, doctors, and pharmacies must be able to count on their distributor to "jump" when an emergency arises requiring unusual volume or special item orders. McKesson has sold itself to its customers as a "we care" company that will do everything it can to resolve emergency situations.

Special orders (those not usually carried at the distribution center) and warehouse business orders (those shipped directly to large corporate clients such as Longs Drugs) make up the remainder of total orders. Although small in number, the warehouse business orders are usually large-volume transactions.

Most routine orders are handled by processing clerks. These workers can be quickly trained and are among the lowest-paid employees in the company. The most skilled and reliable among their number are promoted to customer liaison and inventory clerk positions. These jobs, requiring additional training, carry considerable responsibility. Customer liaisons process special and emergency orders; inventory clerks work directly with filling orders for major corporate clients. Because they are paid about twice what a processing clerk makes, the customer liaisons and inventory clerks represent a significant labor cost to the company, especially when measured against the actual number of orders they handle. Both positions require thorough knowledge of company procedures and resources, quick access to top decision makers within the chain of command, and informed flexibility and creativity in solving emergency situations.

A somewhat elitist culture has developed among the customer liaisons and inventory clerks due to their elevated pay levels and the range of knowledge and skills required for their jobs. They occupy offices separated from the rest of the order department. These employees do not apologize for the fact that they often appear to have little to do during the workday; they rationalize that the company pays them well to "be there," much like firefighters, when emergencies occur. Between emergencies, they consider their time their own. The company has invested approximately $50,000 in specialized training per employee in this work unit.

Insights from the Task Force

One of your members, Bill Jordan, is senior vice president for human resources. His suggestions tend to focus on training and performance evaluation issues: "It all comes down to motivating each employee to do his or her best at all levels of the company. We can best increase efficiency at our distribution center by making sure each employee is well trained for specific job tasks, then measuring their performance regularly and rewarding them accordingly."

Your second member, Alice Morgan, is an upper-level finance manager. "I don't think it's a matter of motivation, Bill. Most of our stockers and order processors work at a steady, if not inspired, pace throughout the day. Only the customer liaisons and inventory clerks seem to have a lot of time on their hands. But you know how that group is—a bunch of prima donnas who like to be heroes for the customer during an emergency but don't do much the rest of the time. I think we can lower costs dramatically without sacrificing customer service by reducing headcount by one-third or more among the customer liaison and inventory clerk positions. If they like playing hero, let the ones who remain play it more often during the workday."

Your perspective, as information systems director, is somewhat different. You recognize that the company is paying an expensive premium for the knowledge the company has put in the heads of the customer liaison and inventory clerk employees. You explain, "I think we need to get a good grasp of what kind of return we're getting on knowledge. Here's what I mean: low-knowledge stocking clerks are performing well and giving us good return for knowledge. But our high-knowledge employees in the customer liaison and inventory clerk positions may not be giving us satisfactory return, in terms of our bottom line, for the knowledge we've invested in them. I think the question is not how to motivate the workforce or reduce their numbers, but instead how to maximize our return on knowledge from our most knowledgable (and most expensive) employees."

For Discussion

Firm conclusions for the McKesson case are, of course, impossible without access to full data. But you can play out initial approaches by thinking through and debating the positions asserted by the three members of the Phase I Task Force. In your discussion, develop descriptions of the kinds of measurement tools you will require prior to proceeding to later stages of investigation, analysis, and recommendations.

7

MEASURING RETURN
ON KNOWLEDGE

We have provided a broad brush-stroke review of some of the most promising approaches to valuing knowledge assets as well as the more traditional approaches to valuing company assets. As we noted in the last chapter, reliable approaches require a common language to discuss the underlying value of an organization's knowledge assets. The knowledge-value-added methodology conforms to this reinforcement and is one of the most robust approaches. Really understanding how the methodology works requires a fairly complete review. Going into more detail here will provide an opportunity to work through some of the more practical issues involved in actually trying to measure knowledge at a granular level. Ultimately, it will be at the granular level that new knowledge measures will provide new raw data for Information Age financial and accounting professionals. Investors, managers, and even customers can rely on such professionals for basic analysis and insight upon which to base their decisions.

KNOWLEDGE-VALUE-ADDED METHODOLOGY

The knowledge-value-added (KVA) methodology addresses a need long recognized by executives and managers by showing how to leverage and measure the knowledge resident in employees, information technology, and core processes. KVA analysis produces a return-on-knowledge (ROK) ratio to estimate the value added by given knowledge assets regardless of where they are located.

The essence of KVA is that knowledge utilized in corporate core processes is translated into numerical form. This translation allows allocation of revenue in proportion to the value added by the knowledge as well as the cost to use that knowledge. Tracking the conversion of knowledge into value while measuring its bottom-line impacts enables managers to increase the productivity of these critical assets. KVA, though based on sophisticated concepts from thermodynamics, is relatively straightforward to apply.

KVA Example

Let's begin with an "average" person who needs to learn how to produce all the outputs of a given company. In a very real sense, then, her knowledge of the company would be the embodiment of the company's value-adding processes including selling, marketing, producing, accounting for, financing, servicing, and maintaining. It is these core processes that add value while converting inputs into outputs that generate the company's revenue.

KVA provides a methodology for allocating revenue and cost to a company's core processes based on the amount of change each produces. Significantly, the knowledge required to make these changes is a convenient way to describe the conversion process.

We define knowledge in a particular way here: It is the know-how required to produce process outputs. This kind of knowledge is proportionate to the time it takes to learn it. We have found learning time to be a quick and convenient way to measure the amount of knowledge contained in any given process.[1] We can put this understanding to the test with a simple example. In the widget company, there is one person, the owner, who makes and sells widgets. This person knows all there is to know in order to make and sell widgets for $1. The owner's sales-production knowledge can be used as a surrogate for the dollar of revenue generated by his application of the core process knowledge. And we can determine how long it would take the widget company owner to transfer all the necessary sales and production knowledge to a new owner. Further, we can use these learning times to allocate the dollar of revenue between the sales and production processes.

For simplicity's sake, let's assume that it takes 100 hours for the new owner to learn the processes, with 70 hours spent learning how to make the widget and 30 hours learning how to sell it. This would indicate that 70 percent of the knowledge and value added was contained in the production process and 30 percent in the sales process. It would follow that $0.70 of the revenue would be allocated to production knowledge and $0.30 to sales knowledge.

All that would be left to do in this example would be to determine how much it costs to use the sales and production knowledge and then we would have a ratio of knowledge value added to knowledge utilization cost. In other words, we can measure return on knowledge (ROK). For the sake of argument, let's assume that the total cost to sell and produce a widget was $0.50: $0.25 for sales and $0.25 for production. The basic approach here is to find out how much it costs to use the sales and production knowledge. In this case, the cost is directly tied to how long the new owner spends performing each process. As it turns out, in this case, the new owner spends the same amount of time to do both and, therefore, the cost to use the knowledge of each process is the same.

Based on our estimates for the distribution of revenue and cost, we would generate an estimate of the ROK. We would conclude that the production process is a more productive use of the knowledge asset (ROK = 0.70/0.25 = 280 percent) than the sales process (ROK = 0.30/0.25 = 120 percent).

---

[1]Other ways to measure amount of knowledge that have been used in the KVA methodology include process instructions, bits, decision points, lines of code, and entries on a sales-order form.

The KVA methodology can be applied at any level in a company. We can conduct rough-cut estimates of the relative return on knowledge of a company's core processes and information technology using the same general approach. Let's say that we want to conduct a quick-and-dirty KVA of the SBC Corporation. We could gather together executives representing the core processes, including sales-order provisioning, marketing, network provisioning, maintenance, and so forth. Each would estimate how long it takes the average person to learn how to produce the outputs of the core areas. For reasons explained below, we'll add one boundary condition: We only have a total of 100 months for our average person to learn everything necessary to generate the annual revenue at SBC. It is normal in such cases to lump support and administrative processes together in one large category or to ignore such processes, depending on the goals of the KVA and for the sake of convenience.

We would not ask the executives to make estimates of the value of their core processes, since discussion could degenerate into a no-win dogfight. Rather, they would be asked to achieve consensus estimates of approximately what portion of the total allotted 100 months our average person should use to learn each core process. These estimates would be weighted by the number of employees in each core process to estimate how frequently the knowledge in a given process is employed in a typical year.

To make a back-of-the-envelope estimate of the knowledge embedded in the information technology of core processes, we could ask for the percentage of the process that is automated. Then the percentage of knowledge for each process, including its supporting information technology, can be calculated by dividing process knowledge by the total amount of knowledge. Revenue is then allocated proportionately.

If we wanted to understand the contribution of information technology, the revenue for each process could be further partitioned into the amount attributable to information technology. The annual budget for each area can be used to estimate the cost to use the given core process knowledge. In most high-tech firms, this is usually the cost for employee salaries and information technology costs. The final step would be to divide the allocated revenue by the cost per core process to determine the relative ROKs.

The revenue attributable specifically to the knowledge embedded in information technology and the cost to use it would provide the ROK for IT within and among processes. This can be quite revealing in that "all IT is not created equal." Some highly automated processes provide much lower ROKs than others in which there is a lower percentage of automation, but IT provides much more "bang for the buck."

Given a common point of reference, learning-time cheating is infrequent because the executives know their estimates can be verified by other knowledge measures such as actual training times and number of process instructions for each process. More importantly, the common reference point for estimation provides a meaningful framework for discussion. And, once the ROKs are calculated, the executives can move forward to prioritize efforts to improve overall company performance.

KVA Theory

KVA is firmly rooted in the Information Age. It allows managers and investors to analyze the performance of corporate knowledge assets in core processes in terms of the

FIGURE 7.1   Fundamental Assumptions of KVA

Underlying Model: Change, Knowledge, and Value are Propotionate

Input   Process   Output

$P(X) = Y$

Fundamental assumptions:

1. If X=Y, no value has been added.
2. "value" ∝ "change"
3. "change" can be measured by the amount of knowledge required to make the change.

So "value" ∝ "change" ∝ "amount of knowledge required to make the change"

returns they generate. This is true whether knowledge is embedded in information technology or employees' heads. This is accomplished by postulating a common unit of knowledge that can be observed in core process and counted in terms of its price and cost. The results of a KVA analysis are ratios that compare the price and cost for these common units of knowledge. Economic components for these ratios are derived from the cash flow from ongoing operations and can be derived contemporaneously with the generation of the cash flow.

The fundamental assumptions can be summarized in Figure 7.1.

The principle of replication states that given that we have the knowledge necessary to produce the change, then we have the amount of change introduced by the knowledge. By definition, if we have not captured the knowledge required to make the changes necessary, we will not be able to produce the output as determined by the process. This tests to determine if the amount of knowledge required to produce an output has been accurately estimated.

For the purposes of simplification, the knowledge audit of KVA methodology can be delineated in seven steps for those who need a more concrete guide. Table 7.1 summarizes three different ways to generate estimates of the value of the knowledge embedded in the core processes of a firm. The Exodus case study that follows will provide a detailed example of how KVA might be applied to helping manage the knowledge in an Internet infrastructure company.

The KVA approach is currently being embedded in the "ProcessEdge"™[2] process modeling tool suite from Intelligent Systems Technology Incorporated. This software will allow analysts to gather and represent KVA data within a process work-flow model as well as monitor the ongoing return on knowledge (ROK) and return on process (ROP).

[2]ProcessEdge is a registered trademark of the Intelligent Systems Technology Corporation and cannot be used without express consent of the company. Visit the website for Intelligent Systems Technology at www.intelsystech.com for a more in-depth review of the software.

TABLE 7.1 THREE APPROACHES TO KVA

Steps	Learning time	Process description	Binary query method
1.	Identify core process and its subprocesses.		
2.	Establish common units to measure learning time.	Describe the products in terms of the instructions required to reproduce them and select unit of process description.	Create a set of binary yes/no questions such that all possible outputs are represented as a sequence of yes/no answers.
3.	Calculate learning time to execute each subprocess.	Calculate number of process instructions pertaining to each subprocess.	Calculate length of sequence of yes/no answers for each subprocess.
4.	Designate sampling time period long enough to capture a representative sample of the core process's final product/service output.		
5.	Multiply the learning time for each subprocess by the number of times the subprocess executes during sample period.	Multiply the number of process instructions used to describe each subprocess by the number of times the subprocess executes during sample period.	Multiply the length of the yes/no string for each subprocess by the number of times this subprocess executes during sample period.
6.	Allocate revenue to subprocesses in proportion to the quantities generated by step 5 and calculate costs for each subprocess.		
7.	Calculate ROK, and interpret the results.		

The knowledge within a process can be represented as learning time, process instructions, or bits. In fact, any approach that satisfies the basic KVA assumptions will work.[3] Based on the fundamental assumption of KVA, the correlation between any two or more estimates should be at a high level to ensure an accurate estimate. This simple matched correlation measures the reliability of an estimate.[4]

KVA: EXODUS COMMUNICATIONS INC.

The following is an example of how KVA can be applied to a company in the Internet infrastructure marketplace. The same general approach can be extended to any company. The KVA methodology is generic and robust enough to be applicable to companies and core processes in any industry.

---

[3]Others have used Jackson Structured Diagrams, Hay knowledge points, service order entries, or lines of code for rough-cut estimates of the amount of knowledge embedded in a process. The critical constraint is that the same referent point or approach be used to estimate all the knowledge in a process or company in order to make common comparisons among the process performance return ratios.

[4]The normal rules of mathematics apply here so that, for example, if one of the subprocess estimates of knowledge is orders of magnitude higher than the others, the correlation will be very high due to a reduction of the variances among the other estimates that are being correlated.

EXODUS COMMUNICATIONS INC. FINANCIAL SUMMARY

Price	52-week range	Shares outstanding (MM)	EPS 99A	EPS 2000E	P/E	Market capitalization
$34	$15–$89	412.4	$(0.36)	$(0.6)	NM	24,820.26 million

NM=not meaningful.

Exodus is a leading provider of web hosting services. The company offers a suite of services including data center, Internet access, and managed services.

1. Exodus is a typical Internet infrastructure company that cannot be meaningfully evaluated by the traditional financial ratios and multiples methods; for example, the P/E ratio is not derivable because the company has no positive net income.
2. The price-to-book value of Exodus is 44.59 while the industry average for this ratio is only 16.69 and the S&P 500 is 9.66. The price-to-tangible value of Exodus is 67.99 while the industry average is only 20.51 and the S&P 500 is 12.77.[5] This means that Exodus stock is being valued more richly relative to the value of its assets than is the case for the S&P 500. It's a good example to illustrate that most of the value of the company is derived from the underlying knowledge assets embedded in the company structure and culture, which is not reflected on the traditional accounting statement.

Company Description

Founded in 1994, Exodus Communications™ has been a pioneer in the Internet data center market. The company offers system and network management solutions, along with technology professional services for customers' websites. Exodus delivers its services from geographically distributed Internet data centers that are connected through a high-performance dedicated and redundant backbone network. The company's tailored solutions are designed to integrate with existing enterprise systems architectures and to enable customers to outsource the monitoring, administration, and optimization of their equipment, applications, and overall Internet operations. Exodus is publicly traded on the Nasdaq National Market under the ticker symbol EXDS.

As of December 31, 1999, the company had over 2,200 customers under contract and managed over 27,000 customer servers worldwide. The company's customers represent a variety of industries, ranging from Internet leaders to major enterprise customers. Yahoo!, USA TODAY.com, weather.com, priceline.com, British Airways, and Nordstrom are just a few of the companies selecting Exodus as their complex Web hosting provider.[6]

[5]Price-to-book value is a theoretical comparison of the value of the company's stock to the value of assets it owns (free and clear of debt). Price to tangible book is similar to price to book, except that we subtract the value of intangibles such as goodwill from book value. Both figures are quoted from www.marketguide.com as of October 31, 2000.

[6]The foregoing information can be found at www.marketguide.com.

Exodus currently operates Internet data centers located in nine metropolitan areas in the United States: Atlanta, Austin, Boston, Chicago, Los Angeles, New York, Seattle, Silicon Valley, and Washington, D.C. In addition, the company opened its first Internet data center outside of the United States in the London metropolitan area in June 1999 and the second in Tokyo, Japan, in December 1999.

Exodus offers three types of services:

1. Internet server hosting.
2. Network solutions.
3. System management and monitoring services.

Current Issues

Exodus Communications currently has three areas of concern:

1. **Decreasing profit margin:** Bandwidth of the Network Solutions and the co-location of Internet Service Hosting are rapidly becoming commodities with smaller and smaller margins as a result of increased competition and the maturation of the industry.
2. **Expansion opportunity:** Exodus's core customers are mostly "blue chip" Fortune 500 companies due to the limited amount of time and sales staff resources. There are opportunities for small customers that require simple and standardized solutions. The current process of service selection and network architecture and design (NAD) is very labor intensive and takes up lots of resources, which makes further expansion difficult.
3. **Emerging competition:** The emerging competition in the industry will lower the average revenue per user of Exodus's customers.

The goal of the exercise is to identify the area for focus on increasing revenue from existing knowledge assets, rather than just cutting cost. The following is an example of how KVA could be applied to Exodus on both the aggregate and the operation levels to measure the value of knowledge created in its core and subprocesses.

Aggregate-Level KVA

A rough-cut estimate KVA on Exodus Communications Inc. is targeted at the aggregate level of analysis. On one hand, the top executives can benchmark the company's use of knowledge assets against other industries. On the other hand, management can look at the level of performance in the company's core processes before deciding how to improve performance.

Assumptions and Methodology   The KVA team would interview process subject matter experts (SMEs), make observations, and talk with process employees and managers to obtain average learning-time estimates and the number of roughly equivalent process instructions required to complete each subprocess. Some of the numbers for the aggregate-level analysis, such as number of employees and expenses, were annualized figures derived from the 1999 financial statement.

1. Determine the core areas—We would gather together the various executives of the core processes in Exodus. Then they would be asked to categorize the company's functions at the aggregate level: Management, Sales and General Administration (S&GA), and Operation. These three functions would be the aggregate of all core processes in the company.
   a. Management includes finance and strategic management.
   b. S&GA includes all supporting functions such as human resources, public relations, and marketing.
   c. Operations includes sales support and design, service selection and network architecture design (NAD), procurement, integration, troubleshooting, and final testing.

   These categorizations are in line with how the accounting cost figures were reported in their annual financial statement.

2. Gather the data on the amount of knowledge embedded in each core area using the learning time approach.
   a. Ranking. Executives from the company would be asked to rank the three above-mentioned areas in terms of hardest to easiest to learn or most to least complex to learn. This ranking method creates a framework to guide the executives to make a first-cut analysis of the underlying amount of knowledge created in each area. It also offers a knowledge estimate that, a priori, is assumed to correlate with the 100-month learning time estimate. The level of the correlation is an indication of the accuracy of the estimate.
   b. Learning time estimation. Executives would then be asked to estimate how long it would take the average person to learn how to produce the outputs of each core area using the 100-month approach. There is a total of only 100 months for an average person to learn everything in the above areas necessary to generate the annual revenue at Exodus. The executives have to estimate the time an average person would use, of the total allotted 100 months, to learn each core process.

3. Weight the amount of knowledge executed in the process.
   a. Determine the number of employees within each core area.
   b. Ask for the percentage of the process that is automated. To truly understand the knowledge embedded in the process, we have to talk to the process subject matter experts to tell us precisely what we need to know to produce the information technology's output within the subprocess under review.
   c. Calculate the percentage of knowledge contained in each process, including its supporting technology. The amount of knowledge in each process is equal to relative learning time multiplied by the number of employees + automation. Then revenue can be allocated proportionately based on this percentage.
   d. Determine the annual budget for each core process or area used in the analysis to generate the cost estimates.

e. Calculate the ROK ratio to estimate the value added by given knowledge assets in each process.

Table 7.2 represents our annualized high-level aggregate view of Exodus's 1999 performance. Each entry of the table is described in the following paragraphs.

In column 1 we identify the core areas of Exodus Communications. The three high-level core areas are categorized as S&GA, Operations, and Management.

In column 2 we rank the areas in terms of the most difficult to the easiest to learn, 1 being the easiest and 3 the hardest. In the table below, S&GA is the easiest area to learn and Operations is the hardest.

In column 3 we assume that it takes 100 months for an average person to learn the three areas. Executives are asked to allocate the 100 months of learning time between these three areas based on an average person. For example, S&GA is the easiest area to learn and takes an average person 20 months out of 100 months to learn all processes in the S&GA area. This approach can keep the executives within the conceptual framework of quantifying the amount of knowledge contained in each function. This figure should correlate with the ranking in column 2. If the two figures don't correlate highly, we will

TABLE 7.2   HIGH-LEVEL AGGREGATE KVA ANALYSIS

Col. 1	Col. 2	Col. 3	Col. 4	Col. 5	Col. 6	Col. 7	Col. 8	Col. 9	Col. 10	Col. 11
Core areas	Rank in terms of difficult to learn (1=easiest, 3=hardest)	Relative learning time (total = 100 months)	Number of employees	Percentage of auto-mation	Amount of knowledge embedded in auto-mation	Total amount of knowledge	Percentage of knowledge allocation	Annual revenue allocation (in millions of U.S. dollars)	Annual expense (in millions of U.S. dollars)	ROK
S&GA	1	20	855	80%	13,680	30,780	34.18%	$ 82.7	$118.8[a]	70%
Operations	3	45	600	60	16,200	43,200	47.98	116.1	197.2[b]	59
Manage-ment	2	35	255	80	7,140	16,065	17.84	43.2	51.0[c]	85
Total		100	1,710[d]		37,020	90,045	100%	$242.0		

[a]Based on 1999 financial statements, S&GA includes two items: (1) general and administrative expenses ($43 million) are primarily comprised of salaries and benefits for administrative and management information systems personnel, consulting fees, recruiting fees, and travel expenses; and (2) the marketing expenses are defined as salaries, commissions, and benefits for our marketing and sales personnel, printing and advertising costs, public relations costs, consultants' fees, and travel and entertainment expenses ($75.8 million).

[b]Based on 1999 financial statements, Operations expenses comprise the costs for salaries and benefits for customer service and operations personnel (customer service personnel, network engineers, and professional services personnel), depreciation and amortization, rent, consultants' fees, network and local telecommunications circuits, interconnections to other networks, repairs and utilities related to the Internet data centers and other sites, and costs of third-party equipment sold or rented to customers. The total was $197.2 million.

[c]Based on an average of $200,000 annual compensation for each management-level executive, a total of 225 management employees equals a total of $51 million as management compensation.

[d]The number 1,710 is the total number of employees worldwide in 1999 as stated in Exodus's 1999 financial statement.

ask the executives to reconsider and re-estimate. The theory predicts that figures in column 2 and column 3 should be 100 percent correlated. However, given the fact that no estimate will ever be perfect, there will always be some measurement error. We have found that the level of correlation should reach a minimum of 85 percent to be acceptable by most executives for the rough-cut, aggregated estimation and 95 percent for the more detailed core process analyses.

In column 4 the number of employees is a rough-cut way of "weighing" knowledge in the core areas for the annualized period. The actual number of executions of knowledge may vary and this issue should be addressed when discussing the reasonableness of the employee-weighting method with executives familiar with the core areas. In Exodus, there are a total of 255 people in the Management area, which represents the number of times the knowledge embedded in the management function area is executed. If we don't have the exact figures of total employees in each area, percentage of employees distributed in each area can be used.

In column 5 the percentage of automation is the estimated amount of knowledge contained in the information technology systems that support these core functions. Executives will be asked to assign a percentage of automation in each core function. The percentage is based on an estimation of how long it would take the average person to learn how to perform the instructions manually that are currently performed by the IT. If we remove the automation, it is the amount of knowledge used to produce the same output as is produced with the automation.

Remember, we need the amount of knowledge embedded in the IT but not the time and cost it takes to execute the knowledge to obtain the output. The time used to produce the same output is an estimate of the cost of using the knowledge embedded in the automation.

In column 6 we calculate the amount of knowledge embedded in automation, which is the learning time (column 3) multiplied by the number of employees (column 4) multiplied by the percentage of automation (column 5).

S&GA	$20 \times 855 \times 80\% = 13,680$
Operations	$45 \times 600 \times 60\% = 16,200$
Management	$35 \times 255 \times 80\% = 7,140$

In column 7 we calculate the total amount of knowledge, which is the learning time (column 3) multiplied by the number of employees (column 4) plus the automation (column 6).

S&GA	$20 \times 855 + 13,680 = 30,780$
Operations	$45 \times 600 + 16,200 = 43,200$
Management	$35 \times 255 + 7,140 = 16,065$

In column 8 we calculate the amount of knowledge allocated to each functional area:

S&GA	$(30,780/90,045) \times 100\% = 34.18\%$
Operations	$(43,200/90,045) \times 100\% = 47.98\%$
Management	$(16,065/90,045) \times 100\% = 17.84\%$

Total amount of knowledge is the total value surrogate of the annual revenue ($242 million). In column 9 annual revenue is allocated based on the percentage of the amount of knowledge embedded in each stage in terms of total knowledge.

S&GA	$242 × 34.18% = $82.7 million
Operations	$242 × 47.98% = $116.1 million
Management	$242 × 17.84% = $43.2 million

Column 10 captures the cost used to generate the outputs of the process.

S&GA	$118.8 million includes the general administrative costs and marketing expenses
Operations	$197.2 million
Management	$51 million

In column 11 we calculate return on knowledge (ROK), which is the allocated revenue (column 9) divided by the cost to use this knowledge (column 10).

S&GA	$ 82.7/$118.8 = 70%
Operations	$116.1/$197.2 = 59%
Management	$ 43.2/$ 51 = 85%

ROK is the ratio of revenue allocated to each core area compared to its corresponding expenses. By comparing the expenses and revenues associated with the knowledge asset, an internal hurdle rate can be computed to compare efficiency in performance of the core areas. In the above example, Exodus's ROK in the three core function areas are less than one because it has not generated positive net income.

Management Implication   Among the three core function areas, the performance of Operations (59 percent) is relatively low as compared to S&GA (70 percent) and Management (85 percent). To take constructive actions to make the company profitable, the KVA analysis can identify the area(s) where the company can be more effective in exploiting its knowledge resources to generate outputs more effectively and efficiently.

To investigate which area in Operations needs improvement, we must go into the core processes to analyze the distribution and contribution of knowledge. Currently, the sales provisioning process is one of the core processes in Exodus's Operations. It presents a major opportunity for further business expansion with the explosive growth in demand for data storage. However, it is also the area where customer turnaround is the slowest due to lack of automation. The costs of expansion in terms of the sales provisioning process are accelerating. Five out of the six subprocesses of sales provisioning fall within the Operations area. The lower ROK in the Operations area has confirmed management's guess and intuition that the sales provisioning process is one of the areas needing improvement.

To reassure investors that management is tackling the biggest problem area, the sales provisioning area was selected for further KVA analysis. The sales provision process includes six subprocesses: sales support and design, service selection and NAD, procurement, integration, troubleshooting, and final testing. All of these subprocesses fall into the Operations area, except the sales support function.

KVA: Sales Provisioning Process

Assumptions and Methodology

1. Data center: Exodus has a total of 22 Internet data centers worldwide. The operations cost and process structure are based on the El Segundo center located in Los Angeles. We assume that all centers are staffed and operated more or less the same way.
2. Learning time and process instruction approach: In addition to learning time, the process instruction approach is another way to measure the amount of knowledge required to produce process outputs. The amount of knowledge required is proportionate to the number of process instructions pertaining to each process.

The learning time, as well as the process instructions, will serve as an estimate for the amount of knowledge contained in each subprocess and should be defined in terms of roughly equal complexity. For example, instructing a person to paint the door green may be less complex than instructing a person to make the customer happy. Generating two independent estimates of knowledge is useful in that it allows an estimate of the accuracy and the reliability of knowledge estimates by making a matched correlation test among the two. The higher the correlation, the better the estimates.

Seven Steps of KVA on Sales Provisioning Process   Step one is to identify the core and subprocesses. The Exodus core sales provisioning process involved six processes: sales support and design, service selection and NAD, procurement, integration, troubleshooting, and final testing. (See Table 7.3, column 1.)

In step two we establish a common definition of learning time for the six processes under review. We would ask the subject matter experts (SMEs) to describe the process instructions for producing the outputs of the six subprocesses. We also would ask the SMEs to estimate how long it would take to teach an "average" person to learn to produce the outputs. The learning time estimate indicated that a total of approximately 2,000 weeks were required to learn the whole sequence of how to execute each subprocess.

In step three we calculate the total time to learn how to execute each subprocess.

1. Learning time approach: we calculate the total time to learn how to execute each subprocess. Given that there were a total of 2,000 weeks to learn how to execute the six processes, the distribution of learning time was as follows: sales required 240 weeks, service selection and NAD required 400 weeks, procurement required 60 weeks, integration required 500 weeks, troubleshooting required 500 weeks, and final testing required 300 weeks (Table 7.3, column 2).
2. Process instruction approach: We need to identify a common language to describe the subprocesses in terms of the process instructions required to produce the out-

TABLE 7.3   KVA ON THE SALES PROVISIONING PROCESS

Column 1	Column 2	Column 3	Column 4	Column 5	Column 6	Column 7	Column 8	Column 9	Column 10
Sub-process	Learning time (weeks)	Number of employees	Amount of knowledge embedded in IT (35%)	Total amount of knowledge	Percentage of knowledge allocation	Annual revenue allocation (in millions)	Process costs (in millions)	ROK	ROK on industry average
Sales Service selection and NAD	240	8	672	2,592	15%	$13.7	$12.2	112%	100%
Procurement	400	8	1,120	4,320	25	22.8	24.3	94	150
Integration	60	5	105	405	2.5	2.3	3.0	77	150
Trouble-shooting	500	5	875	3,375	20	18.3	20.3	90	80
Final testing	500	6	1,050	4,050	23.5	21.4	19.0	1.13	1
	300	6	630	2,430	14	12.8	6.4	200	125
Total	2,000	38		17,172	100%	$91.3	$85.2	107%	

puts. For example, the sales support and design function required 240 learning weeks or 280 process instructions to produce the output.

The process instruction estimates for the six subprocesses correlated above 89 percent with the corresponding learning time estimates (Table 7.4). Given the high level of correlation, there would be a fair degree of confidence that both learning times and process task estimates were a reasonably accurate measure of the same underlying amounts of knowledge embedded in each subprocess. Because of the high correlation we decided to use only the learning times for the ROK estimates.

In step four we designate a sampling time period long enough to capture a representative sample of the compound processes' final product/service output. In this case, the annualized period was used, so number of employees was the weighting factor.

In step five we multiply the learning time for each subprocess by the number of times the subprocess executes during the sample period. In this case, we multiplied the number of employees (Table 7.3, column 3) by the learning time (column 2). Then we added the amount of automation (column 4) to derive the total amount of knowledge used in the subprocess (column 5). The total percentage of knowledge is proportionately allocated to each subprocess in column 6 and the total amount of revenue for each subprocess is also allocated in column 7.

In step six (see Table 7.5) we calculate the cost to execute each subprocess based on the assumption that the total of 22 worldwide data centers share the same cost structure as a typical one in El Segundo. This assumption can be checked for accuracy in further discussions with the appropriate SMEs and executives. The annual cost for each subprocess is represented in column 8. In this case, the primary determinant of cost was

TABLE 7.4   LEARNING TIME AND PROCESS INSTRUCTIONS APPROACH CORRELATION

Subprocess	Learning time (weeks)	Process instructions
Sales	240	280
Service selection and NAD	400	400
Procurement	60	200
Integration	500	560
Troubleshooting	500	400
Final testing	300	280
Total	2,000	2,120

Correlation	Learning time	Process instructions
Learning time	1	1
Process instructions	0.8903	1

the number of employees working in each area and this was used to allocate cost with other general expenses (real estate, equipment, power, etc.) equally divided among the subprocesses.[7]

In step seven we compute the ROKs for each subprocess using revenue allocated for each subprocess (Table 7.3, column 7) as the numerator and cost for each subprocess (column 8) for the denominator. The resulting returns on knowledge are represented in column 9, with hypothetical average benchmark comparisons from other companies in the industry represented in column 10.

The following is a partial list of the beneficial ways that KVA analyses have been used in a wide variety of companies. Creative managers and executives will find new ways adapted to their particular needs.

- Tool to control operations: Management needs current and dynamic feedback to steer the company to profitability. Traditional financial tools provide a set of figures with no indication to management what kinds of returns each core area or process is providing. The results of a KVA analysis are ratios that compare the price and the cost for these common units of knowledge across core areas and processes. The economic data for these ratios are derived from cash flow from ongoing operations and can be derived contemporaneously with the generation of cash flow. KVA therefore provides contemporaneous feedback to the company's performance about how well the company is self-organizing and adapting to the dynamic market environment to enhance value for both shareholders and customers. It is a tool to direct allocation of knowledge assets and capital resources.
- New set of raw data: KVA uses a new set of raw data that can be validated and reliably used to measure the performance of corporate knowledge assets. The cal-

[7]For purposes of the rough-cut method, we use loaded labor costs for the outputs of each subprocess. These estimates were derived from approximations of how long it took process employees to generate the necessary outputs. For instance, the salesperson takes an average of three months to close one sales deal. The monthly salary of the salesperson is $15,400 and the whole process costs $46,200 ($15,400 × 3). The process costs of the whole company based on 22 data centers are $12.2 million annually (column 6 in Table 7.5).

TABLE 7.5   SUBPROCESS COST CALCULATION

Column 1	Column 2	Column 3	Column 4	Column 5	Column 6
Cost for executing the knowledge	Execution time (months)	Monthly rate	Process cost	Process cost of each data center on an annual basis	Process cost of the whole company (total of 22 data centers) (in millions)
Sales	3	$15,400	$46,200	$ 554,400	$12.2
Service selection and NAD	12	7,680	92,160	1,105,920	24.3
Procurement	3	3,840	11,520	138,240	3.0
Integration	20	3,840	76,800	921,600	20.3
Troubleshooting	15	4,800	72,000	864,000	19.0
Final testing	5	4,800	24,000	288,000	6.4
Total				$3,872,160	$85.2

culation of ROP and ROK will help avoid subjective manipulation. However, it should be remembered that all calculations are subject to manipulation, but when both value and cost are matched for given core areas and processes, manipulation becomes more difficult.

- Increase in employee's understanding of the value of the production process: KVA is easy to understand. It helps employees, even persons not familiar with finance and accounting, to understand the value they are contributing to the core processes and the company bottom line. Such a concept helps to convert the company's strategy into tangible objectives for employees such as setting a return-based hurdle rate for their performance.
- Enhancement of employees' productivity: KVA helps to create a framework throughout the company that encourages managers and employees to think and behave like owners. In addition, it provides a framework for the Information Age managers to more explicitly understand how to manage knowledge assets.
- Efficient resource allocation: At the operational level, this approach helps to increase the shareholder's value through increased efficiency in allocation of knowledge assets and capital resources. In many companies, all effort is diverted to cut cost while ignoring revenue; value at all levels has been ignored because, in the past, there has been no explicit way to allocate revenue to core process activities.
- Tool to measure manager's performance: KVA makes top managers responsible for the operations over which they have control. Value is created by knowledge that is affected by their decisions rather than by external market factors that they feel they cannot control, for example, the market price of the company's share or product.
- Benchmark of the company with industry or competitors: KVA offers a value-based method for comparing companies' knowledge asset performance within an industry.

- A starting point to improve financial and business policy: When companies examine themselves as a set of knowledge assets and knowledge outputs, companies can identify and invest in the processes, technologies, and people that provide the greatest return.

CONCLUSION

The KVA methodology has been applied in over 100 companies within the last nine years. The results have led some executives to totally reexamine the way they view their businesses and to redesign and develop strategic directions appropriately. In some cases, such as the Courthouse Athletic Club, it has led to relatively simple changes that not only saved the company from bankruptcy but led to the best numbers in its market segment. KVA also has been used in companies where the executive team did nothing as a result. KVA analysis alone is not enough to sway executives to embrace a new knowledge-based paradigm for running their businesses. However, with the relatively concrete quantitative analyses produced from a KVA analysis, it is a start. Numbers alone cannot change an executive's world view, but the better these numbers reflect real business performance, the more likely executives will be to change their views. Regardless of the approach taken, such analyses must objectively quantify the performance of core knowledge assets deployed in processes and tie them unambiguously to the corporate bottom line to be successful.

No measurement methodology, however useful, can replace the creative insights, judgment, and intuition of managers and investors. KVA is no exception to this rule and is best used as a decision support tool.

This raw unit of measure may seem especially intractable because there is no generally agreed-upon "currency" for knowledge. Imagine, for a moment, the seeming impossibility of finding a raw unit of economic measure at a time in human history when some cultures were trading in salt, some in shells, and some in goats. We are at a similar juncture with regard to defining a raw unit measure of knowledge. The effort to find such a measure is not quixotic. The absence of an underlying, agreed-upon value system for knowledge makes any definition of a raw unit of measurement difficult. But only by positing such unit descriptions and applying them to the valuing process will we make progress in achieving a widely recognized, validated, and supported currency for knowledge measurement.

QUESTIONS FOR REVIEW

1. What are the potential limitations of the KVA approach?
2. How does using the KVA methodology allow the knowledge management analyst to get executives "on the same page" when reviewing how well their organizations' core processes are performing?
3. When is it appropriate to conduct a high-level corporate KVA and when is it appropriate to conduct a more detailed KVA?

4. What are the benefits of performing a KVA in developing and testing a knowledge management strategy?
5. How can you measure the reliability of the learning time and process instruction estimates?
6. How can work-flow tools help in conducting KVAs?
7. What would it take for KVA to meet the requirements of the accounting and finance communities from a measurement perspective?

ELECTRONIC TOOLS FOR KNOWLEDGE MANAGEMENT[1]

Identifying, nurturing, and harvesting knowledge is a principal concern in the Information Age. Effective use of knowledge-facilitating tools and techniques is critical, and a number of computational tools have been developed.

While numerous techniques are available, it remains difficult to analyze or compare the specific tools. In part, this is because knowledge management is a young discipline. The arena is evolving rapidly as more people enter the fray and encounter new problems.

In addition, new technologies support applications that were impossible before. Moreover, the multidisciplinary character of knowledge management combines several disciplines, including business and management, computer science, cybernetics, and philosophy. Each of these fields may lay claim to the study of knowledge management, and the field is frequently defined so broadly that anything can be incorporated. Finally, it is difficult to make sense of the many tools available. A recent LookSmart.com search produced a list of nearly 100 software providers. Each of the software packages employs unique visions and aims to capture its share of the market.

This chapter outlines a framework for analyzing and comparing knowledge management tools. In these pages, we detail what we mean by knowledge management tools and propose a framework for analyzing them based on *knowledge structure* and *knowledge services*. Then we apply the proposed framework to compare some current tools.

SCOPING THE PROBLEM

One of the most difficult issues in discussing knowledge management tools is to define what they are and are not. We realize there is no single right answer to this question, but we propose an answer in what follows.

---

[1]This chapter was written by Dr. Andre Valente and Tom Housel.

What Is Knowledge?

One of the central problems in defining knowledge management tools is the existence of radically different views on what knowledge is (and thus how it is managed). We begin with the view that knowledge is something that enables a person or machine to solve problems of a certain type. This premise excludes facts about a specific instance of a problem (which we call *information*), but includes facts about general types of elements in a domain. Like any other, this definition is controversial, but our analysis demonstrates why we have chosen to use it.

In addition, there is a fundamental distinction between knowledge and "knowledge sources." A document that explains how to troubleshoot a certain model of keyboard certainly *contains* knowledge in the sense that someone can read that document and solve problems with the knowledge extracted. In our view, the document is a *knowledge source* but by itself it is not knowledge. The same holds for people. They contain knowledge and therefore are knowledge sources.

In contrast, a set of logical rules or a computer program that can be used to solve the problem is *knowledge*. This distinction is fundamental to understanding the different types of knowledge management tools.

Infrastructure vs. Services

In addition, we maintain that tools like intranets, extranets, and portals are not knowledge management tools per se. They do not offer any knowledge management *services* but only an *infrastructure* on which these services are offered. An analogy with computer networks may be helpful. Network cabling connects all the computers in your office with Ethernet cables. Ethernet cards consist of the basic infrastructure needed to create a network but are not *sufficient* to establish a network. The network is operational only when you install programs that offer *services* users can employ to perform a task. Without the program and attendant services, the network is useless.

Similarly, intranets, extranets, and portals provide the infrastructure to facilitate communication, but by themselves they are not knowledge management tools. Alone they do not perform knowledge management services.

Computational Tools

A large part of the literature on knowledge management deals with the social and organizational problems encountered in establishing knowledge management processes. These are undoubtedly relevant concerns, but we do not regard them as tools. By tools we mean *computational* tools such as software that support the main tasks in knowledge management.

Of course, there is a gray area with respect to tools that explicitly model the knowledge management process, working at the meta-level. We will consider these to be knowledge management tools because they are systems that support the knowledge management process and thus fit the proposed definition.

KSS: KNOWLEDGE STRUCTURE AND SERVICES

We propose that two dimensions are central to analyzing and comparing knowledge management tools: *knowledge structure* and *knowledge services.* These two dimensions can be used to form a matrix in which specific knowledge management tools are positioned.

Knowledge Structure

There is a wide range of levels of formalization or *structure* in the ways knowledge is represented in knowledge management systems, as shown in Figure 8.1.

The knowledge forms listed in Figure 8.1 are not discrete, or exhaustive, and other levels could be added. Examples of the knowledge forms are:

- Creative knowledge is intrinsically nonformalizable and may not be representable in any formalization.
- Audio and video contain multiple "streams" of knowledge such as music, voices, faces, and objects. Humans recognize these features but creating machine recognition is an extremely complex undertaking.
- A raw text document is the formal equivalent of an audio track and is comparable to natural language that is also difficult for machines to understand.

FIGURE 8.1 Dimensions of knowledge structure. From top to bottom we increase the formalization and precision of knowledge, while from bottom to top we accommodate more informality and ambiguity. Knowledge forms toward the top end are relatively easy for people to create and update, while knowledge forms toward the bottom increasingly demand knowledge engineering and incremental analysis.

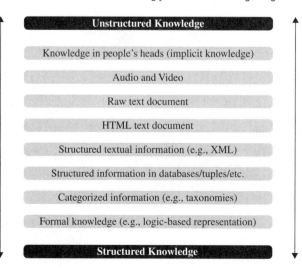

- In contrast, an HTML document with markup tags can display the texts' structure. Irregularities in the structure can aid in interpreting the content. For example, "wrappers" convert structural marks into semantic descriptions and may interpret the HTML markups on a country name to display its population, as in the pages of the CIA factbook.
- Structured documents using formats like XML or its ancestor, SGML, explicate the semantics implicit in HTML markups. For example, instead of deducing that a certain tag such as <H1>USA</H1> indicates that "USA" is the name of a country, an XML document could contain a tag such as <country name>USA</country name> that makes the text an explicit country name.
- XML documents are linear representations of "tuples" of data, the essence of information stored in databases. For example, a sequence of tags can contain a <population> tag inside a <country> tag to indicate a relationship between the country and its population. This facilitates efficient storage and retrieval of that information, but the tags are invisible to users.
- Categorized information is at roughly the same level as structured information in databases. Taxonomies such as the ones we use in biology are examples of categorized information. This kind of knowledge is used extensively by directory sites such as Yahoo! to provide taxonomies of concepts, ideas, or subjects.
- We use the term "formal knowledge" in the mathematical sense. Logical statements such as theorems and equations are used in a very rigorous way to make sure all semantics are explicit and rules are followed. This makes it easy for machines to interpret this kind of knowledge.

The level of structure in the knowledge directly affects the amount of automated processing that can be performed because more structured knowledge employs powerful semantics. As a result, it is much easier to process the information contents of an XML than an HTML page.

Managing highly unstructured knowledge requires more structured descriptions of the content, just as video indexing employs close-captioned text and HTML pages are indexed by metatags. Most knowledge found on the Web falls near the top of the scale, and it is no coincidence that most knowledge management tools concentrate on this range.

In addition, semantics and interpretation of less structured forms of knowledge depend on contextual knowledge. Raw text files representing a speech eliminate many of the possible ambiguities in speech recognition. In this case, contextual knowledge about the subject, the person, and the person's voice are used to "reduce" less structured forms of knowledge to more structured forms. After the transformation process, we need less additional contextual knowledge to be able to use the desired knowledge.

Knowledge Services

Another useful dimension is the range of *services* knowledge management tools provide. By services, we mean tasks or activities in handling knowledge that can be at least

FIGURE 8.2   Major Types of Services Provided by Knowledge Management Tools

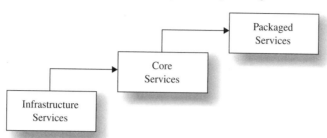

partially automated. While not all services are comparable, analysis of the knowledge services provided includes things ranging from e-mail to intranets to data mining and customer relationship management. To make sense of these disparate services, knowledge services may be divided into three main types: infrastructure services, core services, and packaged services. These services build on one another such that packaged services make use of core services, which employ infrastructure services. For example, software that provides core services depends upon infrastructure services. This relationship is displayed in Figure 8.2.

Each main type of service contains several major or typical services supporting knowledge management tools. The lists are not exhaustive, but rather present a collection of typical offerings.[2]

Infrastructure Services

Infrastructure services are usually needed to implement any such knowledge management solution. Five basic types of infrastructure services are listed in Figure 8.3.

- **Communication services** enable electronic communication between users through e-mail, file transfer, chats, and similar vehicles.
- **Collaboration services** allow for groups of people to communicate through online meetings, shared whiteboards, and discussion groups, as well as directory services. Building upon communications services, these tools are also known as groupware, and the best known example is Lotus Notes.
- **Translation services** transform knowledge from one file format to another or from one language to another.
- **Workflow management services** define workflows and support online execution and control of workflows. Typical applications allow users to execute and enter the results of subtasks and view the status of other subtasks. Workflow management services build upon collaboration services.

---

[2]In fact, this layered definition of services could be used as an approach to creating a taxonomy of services offered by knowledge management tools.

FIGURE 8.3   Infrastructure Services

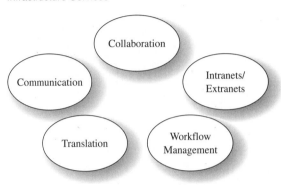

- **Intranets and extranets** include other infrastructure services. Intranets are Web-based applications restricted to specific organizations while extranets connect several organizations by providing access from one organization to another's content and services. Both intranets and extranets extend or aggregate other infrastructure services and add additional services such as user management, personalization, and configuration.
- **Intelligent agents** are software components that are capable of accomplishing tasks on behalf of a user. They go beyond "information on demand" and make selected decisions based on predetermined environmental scanning methods. They can also summarize relevant data by aggregating and performing some synthesizing functions before presenting it to executive decision makers.

Intelligent agents include "interface agents," which act like personal assistants collaborating with a user in the same work environment; mobile agents, which roam wide-area networks and interact with foreign hosts to gather information; information/internet agents, which help manage, manipulate, or collate information from distributed sources; and reactive agents, which respond to the environment in which they are embedded.

Core Services

Core services define knowledge management solutions because they explicitly and directly access knowledge repositories. Figure 8.4 shows how these core services are built around core processes of creating, organizing, and using a knowledge repository. Different core processes involve people or systems with different roles, including knowledge producer, holder, organizer, and user. Knowledge producers create knowledge while knowledge holders learn from other sources. Knowledge organizers work like librarians and allow producers to add knowledge in an orderly fashion to facilitate retrieval by users. Knowledge users consume knowledge to execute tasks and processes of their interest.

FIGURE 8.4   Core Knowledge Management Services

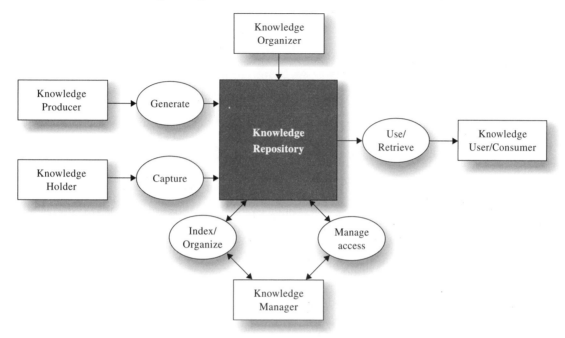

Key features of the five core services include the following:

- **Knowledge generation** services produce knowledge in forms that can be stored in the knowledge repository. Used by knowledge producers, these tools distill, refine, or simply create new knowledge that is then entered into the repository. These tools typically involve some kind of automated learning and include data-mining techniques and pattern recognition. Collaborative creation of a document is an example, and commercial versions include Interscape.com.
- **Knowledge capture** services facilitate addition to repositories. For example, capture tools allow users to enter new documents and may employ meta-information for indexing purposes. A simple example is the "document properties" mechanism of Microsoft Word, which contains information about the document being edited including author, revision number, subject, and date.
- **Knowledge organization (indexing)** services help knowledge managers arrange items in a repository to facilitate retrieval and use. Typical knowledge organization services add to or modify knowledge *about* repository indexes, taxonomies, and directories.
- **Access management services** determine who can access elements of the repository. They control access to the knowledge repository and are usually based on a directory of users. They may restrict who has access by permission levels.

- **Retrieval services** include searching and navigating functions as well as translation, visualization, and integration. They create value by making knowledge available for specific uses and may provide personalization and configuration services.

Packaged Services

Packaged services (see Figure 8.5) aggregate lower-level services to solve specific types of problems such as customer relationship management. Much knowledge management literature concentrates on these packaged services. This focus is attributable to the fact that these types of problems are clearly connected to end-user needs. For example, it is easier for a CIO to justify purchase of customer relationship tools than a search engine.[3]

The literature concentrates on three classes of packaged services.

- **Customer Relationship Management (CRM) services** provide information about a company's clients in an integrated way. They typically allow internal channels to share and add to the same central knowledge base. Siebel and People-Soft are leading providers of CRM services. (CRM is covered in greater depth in Chapter 9.)
- **Business Intelligence services** manage knowledge about competitors and partners. They usually aggregate and provide unified interfaces to information from news agencies, public and private databases, economic and social information, and the World Wide Web. They also filter and classify information into categories.
- **Enterprise Information Portals** are specialized gateways providing access to internal and external sources of knowledge. They provide one-stop access, and typical examples include search engines and My Yahoo! (http://my.yahoo.com).

FIGURE 8.5   Main Types of Packaged Services in the Market Today

---

[3]This is similar to the reason why it is easier to explain the value proposition of an application such as Microsoft Office than it is to explain the value of a technology like Java: It is simply much easier to understand how and why it will be used, and what benefits will be gained from its use (i.e., ultimately, its return on knowledge).

The Knowledge Structure and Services (KSS) Matrix and the KSS Checklist

Different tools provide distinct arrays of services and manage specific types of knowledge. We visualize relationships between knowledge management tools in terms of the types of knowledge they handle and the types of services they offer. Two diagrams display these relationships: the *KSS Matrix* and the *KSS Checklist*. These diagrams position the kinds of solutions provided by given products or vendors. Of course, more complete analysis could include additional elements such as hardware and software platforms, the quality of its customer support, and price.

The KSS Matrix   The KSS Matrix assures that the types of knowledge handled are intimately connected with the core services provided. Tools may support different sets of services for each type of knowledge.

The KSS Matrix is displayed in Figure 8.6. The horizontal axis recognizes the five core knowledge services while the vertical axis displays the eight basic levels of knowledge structure dimension.

One KSS Matrix is used for each tool analyzed. A KSS Matrix is filled by adding small or large squares to each of the cells. Filling a cell indicates that the tool provides a specific service that manipulates knowledge with a given level of structure. The size of the square filling a cell represents the scope of the service offered by the tool. A large square denotes a major offering with a comprehensive set of features, while a small square marks a service that is offered in either a restricted scope or restricted functionality.

The KSS Checklist   The KSS Checklist recognizes services beyond the core services. A checklist is employed because infrastructure and packaged services are inde-

FIGURE 8.6   Basic KSS Matrix to Analyze and Compare Different Tool Offerings

		Knowledge Structure							
		Formal knowledge	Categorized information	Structured information	Structured text	Marked-up text	Raw text	Audio/Video	Implicit knowledge
Core Knowledge Services	Generate								
	Capture								
	Index/Organize								
	Manage access								
	Use/Retrieve								

FIGURE 8.7   Basic KSS Checklist Used to Analyze and Compare Different Tool Offerings

Infrastructure Services	Communication	
	Collaboration	
	Translation	
	Workflow Management	
	Intelligent Agents	
	Intranets/Extranets	
Packaged Services	Enterprise Information Portal	
	Business Intelligence	
	Customer Relationship Management	

pendent of the types of knowledge managed. The KSS Checklist, as shown in Figure 8.7, lists the five infrastructure services and the three packaged services. To the right, we add squares indicating that a service is provided. As with the KSS Matrix, the size of the square represents the scope of the service offered, with a large square indicating major offerings and small squares representing incomplete or restricted offerings.

The KSS Matrix and the KSS Checklist provide quick assessments of each tool and can also be used to compare tools quickly. More importantly, the matrix and checklist can be used to evaluate knowledge management tools. Filling in the diagrams forces users to explore and analyze tools in detail. At the same time, the KSS framework can be used to select tools for specific uses. Specifications can be represented as "target" diagrams for ideal offerings to be matched with the capabilities of specific tools.

USING THE KSS MATRIX AND CHECKLIST TO COMPARE CURRENT KNOWLEDGE MANAGEMENT TOOLS

As examples, this section compares five leading knowledge management tools. We selected tools that represent the range of commercial tools and show the status of current practices.

Our analysis concentrates on specific tools and does not represent the set of tools provided by specific companies.

The five tools we analyze are Documentum 4i, OpenText LiveLink, Autonomy KnowledgeServer, Lotus Notes R5, and PeopleSoft Customer Relationship Management.

Documentum 4i

Documentum 4i[4] is an integrated software suite that serves a large spectrum of services and structures. It is centered on document management, and its core strengths are in

---

[4]http://www.documentum.com.

FIGURE 8.8   KSS Matrix and Checklist for Documentum 4i

		Knowledge Structure								Infrastructure Services		
		Formal knowledge	Categorized information	Structured information	Structured text	Marked-up text	Raw text	Audio/Video	Implicit knowledge			

		Formal knowledge	Categorized information	Structured information	Structured text	Marked-up text	Raw text	Audio/Video	Implicit knowledge
Core Knowledge Services	Generate								
	Capture		■		■	■	■		■
	Index/Organize		■		■	■	■		■
	Manage access		■		■	■	■		■
	Use/Retrieve		■		■	■	■		■

Infrastructure Services	Communication	■
	Translation	
	Collaboration	■
	Intranet/Extranet	■
	Workflow Management	■
Packaged Services	Enterprise Information Portal	■
	Business Intelligence	
	Customer Relationship Management	

dealing with documents. It supports audio/video and taxonomy, as well as some coverage of categorized information. It does not support knowledge generation services or formal knowledge, structured information, or implicit knowledge. The services checklist (Figure 8.8) shows that Documentum 4i is intended to be an Enterprise Information Portal tool, and it supports workflow management and collaboration.

OpenText LiveLink

OpenText LiveLink[5] is also an integrated software suite focused on document management. The KSS Matrix (Figure 8.9) shows that it provides a core set of services to handle document management and structured information from databases. The services checklist shows that LiveLink is an Enterprise Information Portal tool and that it supports translation and collaboration, including discussion groups and group scheduling.

Autonomy KnowledgeServer

Autonomy KnowledgeServer[6] is yet another software suite for content management. In addition, it provides sophisticated services for classifying material based on the content of documents. It is unique in that it covers formal knowledge. We can see that KnowledgeServer's use of learning algorithms facilitates some knowledge generation services. (See Figure 8.10.) Note that it also has some translation and collaboration services but does not incorporate workflow management.

[5]http://www.opentext.com.
[6]http://www.autonomy.com.

FIGURE 8.9   KSS Matrix and Checklist for OpenText LiveLink

Core Knowledge Services / Knowledge Structure	Formal knowledge	Categorized information	Structured information	Structured text	Marked-up text	Raw text	Audio/Video	Implicit knowledge
Generate								
Capture			■	■	■	■	■	
Index/Organize			■	■	■	■	■	
Manage access			■	■	■	■	■	
Use/Retrieve			■	■	■	■	■	

Infrastructure Services	
Communication	■
Translation	■
Collaboration	■
Intranet/Extranet	■
Workflow Management	■

Packaged Services	
Enterprise Information Portal	■
Business Intelligence	
Customer Relationship Management	

FIGURE 8.10   KSS Matrix and Checklist for Autonomy KnowledgeServer

Core Knowledge Services / Knowledge Structure	Formal knowledge	Categorized information	Structured information	Structured text	Marked-up text	Raw text	Audio/Video	Implicit knowledge
Generate	■	■						
Capture	■	■	■	■	■	■	■	■
Index/Organize	■	■	■	■	■	■	■	■
Manage access	■	■	■	■	■	■	■	■
Use/Retrieve	■	■	■	■	■	■	■	■

Infrastructure Services	
Communication	
Translation	■
Collaboration	■
Intranet/Extranet	
Workflow Management	

Packaged Services	
Enterprise Information Portal	■
Business Intelligence	
Customer Relationship Management	

Lotus Notes R5

Lotus Notes R5[7] is virtually synonymous with groupware. This characterizes both its strengths and weaknesses because R5 handles only unstructured types of knowledge. It supports implicit knowledge through use of detailed descriptions of people's information and skills. Lotus R5 does not attempt to be a packaged service as defined here, because it focuses exclusively on collaboration. (See Figure 8.11.)

[7]http://www.lotus.com.

FIGURE 8.11   KSS Matrix and Checklist for Lotus Notes R5

Core Knowledge Services	Knowledge Structure							
	Formal knowledge	Categorized information	Structured information	Structured text	Marked-up text	Raw text	Audio/Video	Implicit knowledge
Generate								
Capture				■	■	■	■	■
Index/Organize				■	■	■	■	■
Manage access				■	■	■	■	■
Use/Retrieve				■	■	■	■	■

Infrastructure Services		
Communication	■
Translation	
Collaboration	■
Intranet/Extranet	■
Workflow Management	

Packaged Services		
Enterprise Information Portal	
Business Intelligence	
Customer Relationship Management	

PeopleSoft Customer Relationship Management

PeopleSoft Customer Relationship Management[8] is a typical vertical solution software that specializes in customer relationship management. PeopleSoft acquired the product when it purchased Vantive, and its "vertical" bias determines the way it provides services all geared toward specific needs of CRM processes. While PeopleSoft CRM supports structured information, it only handles information about customers. This specialization makes it a good choice for CRM, but a poor choice for general knowledge management problems. (See Figure 8.12.)

CONCLUSION

Modern-day alchemy is about turning information into knowledge. Whereas ancient alchemists aimed to turn lead into gold, today's alchemists are turning information into knowledge. The combination of knowledge management tools with databases and knowledge in the minds of employees is fostering knowledge groups, knowledge enterprises, and knowledge industries. These tools are a key component in unleashing the value of knowledge management processes.

The KSS framework provides a convenient way to characterize knowledge management tools by defining the types of knowledge they can handle and the types of services they provide to support knowledge management processes.

The KSS Matrix and the KSS Checklist help visualize the coverage of specific tools and are, therefore, a convenient way to quickly compare and distinguish different tool offerings. They can be used to evaluate specific needs and match them to the services

[8]http://www.peoplesoft.com.

FIGURE 8.12   KSS Matrix and Checklist for PeopleSoft CRM

		Formal knowledge	Categorized information	Structured information	Structured text	Marked-up text	Raw text	Audio/Video	Implicit knowledge
		Knowledge Structure							
Core Knowledge Services	Generate								
	Capture			■	■	■	■	■	■
	Index/Organize			■	■	■	■	■	■
	Manage access			■	■	■	■	■	■
	Use/Retrieve			■	■	■	■	■	■

Infrastructure Services	Communication	■
	Translation	
	Collaboration	■
	Intranet/Extranet	
	Workflow Management	■
Packaged Services	Enterprise Information Portal	
	Business Intelligence	
	Customer Relationship Management	■

provided by available tools. Further, they separate different types of knowledge management tools and avoid comparing apples to oranges.

Services are key elements in understanding knowledge management tools, but complete evaluations should include other aspects. Users should specify the benefits they want to obtain and take into account hardware, software, and budget constraints. Also, more complex tools may require expensive and time-consuming installation and configuration processes.

Above all, electronic tools provide necessary "horsepower" and number-crunching ability to deal with the daunting complexity of real-world situations. As tempting as it is to rush to broad, Platonic theories of what knowledge is and what it does, we may be better served by pursuing an empirical course. The processing path of electronic knowledge measurement and management tools is, in fact, an empirical map or track of knowledge events. Electronic tools are needed to cope with the bewildering number and variety of events and to yield results consistent with the perceptual and cognitive powers of the human mind. In short, electronic tools assess difficult problems and give us simple answers, but we must exercise caution in creating capable tools and in demanding answers that are simple rather than simplistic.

QUESTIONS FOR REVIEW

1. With technology rapidly evolving, how long can we expect knowledge management tools to be useful?
2. Which kinds of knowledge management tools are most likely to evolve and which are most likely to be discarded along the way? Why?

3. Will there be an integrated suite of tools to fulfill most of an organization's knowledge management needs in the near future? What characteristics must such a tool suite include?

4. What will cause a consolidation of knowledge management tool companies? When might this be likely to take place?

5. How might an economic justification for selecting tools be included in the chapter's evaluation framework?

6. What kinds of knowledge management tools are most amenable to the evaluation framework introduced in this chapter?

CASE STUDY: The Informedia Digital Library Project[9]

The Informedia digital library project aims to dramatically advance the means of collecting, storing, and organizing information in digital forms and make it available for searching, retrieval, and processing via communication networks in user-friendly ways. Digital Libraries store electronically formatted materials and organize these materials effectively. As such, this kind of tool promises greater efficiencies in capturing, distributing, retrieving, and managing knowledge in a user-friendly electronic format. The Informedia Digital Library Project is perhaps the leading example of this form of knowledge management tool.

Overview

The Informedia project at Carnegie Mellon University is an exciting knowledge management application. Researchers at the university have developed an "intelligent" motion video database that automatically indexes videos based on sophisticated pattern recognition algorithms, text grammar, and video frames.

Most videos are narrated by actors or narrators, and their speech is converted via voice recognition into text, which is then used to segment the videos. Indexing is by keywords, themes, or context, and videos are segmented by frame so that users can search by scenery, people, vehicles, fires, and other elements.

These indexing techniques provide users sophisticated search techniques that far surpass Internet search engines. Very large video databases may be searched quickly. For example, if the user wants to know how many trees are cut down in the Amazonian rain forest each year, the Informedia video library will find the two-minute segment of a two-hour video on the rain forest that pertains specifically to the number of trees cut down each year.

[9]The Informedia Digital Video Library is a research initiative at Carnegie Mellon University funded by the NSF, DARPA, NASA, and others that studies how multimedia digital libraries can be established and used. Informedia is building a multimedia library that will consist of over 1,000 hours of digital video, audio, images, text, and other related materials.

Voice recognition enables even novice users to navigate without using a keyboard. Informedia assumes that broadband networks are in place so that very powerful computers are not needed to handle video compression and decompression.

A description of the Informedia Digital Video Library from the project team follows.

> Informedia's digital video library is populated by automatically encoding, segmenting and indexing data. Research in the areas of speech recognition, image understanding and natural language processing supports the automatic preparation of diverse media for full-content and knowledge-based search and retrieval. Informedia is one of six Digital Libraries Initiative projects.

Issues

Digital library research concentrates on developing the necessary infrastructure to effectively mass-manipulate information on the World Wide Web. Key technological issues include how to search and display desired selections from and across large collections. The team is investigating segmenting and indexing video, using automatic speech recognition and knowledge about program structure.

Potential business applications include marketing new products, advertising such as yellow pages, policy, work-rules learning and review, training online, on-demand helplines, self-paced learning, and remote site networked learning.[10]

The Informedia project's capabilities are being extended to the commercial world with a number of very promising projects. For example, NetBill aims to provide an extremely secure billing system that is economically feasible for even small purchases on the order of $0.25 to $5.

Developing a very secure billing system for small transactions requires reducing transaction costs, which can be as much as 25 percent of the sales price.

> "NetBill acts as a third party for online transactions and can track payments, just like sending certified mail. And electronic goods transferred are useless unless the sale goes through. First, a merchant sends out the electronic goods, such as software, to the buyer's computer. A confirmation is sent back to the merchant. The merchant then sends the buyer's account information and a decryption key to NetBill's server. NetBill verifies there is money in the buyer's account to pay for the goods then sends the decryption key to unlock the electronic goods. But what makes NetBill better than other systems is that its 'keys,' or electronic password cards, are not shared, according to Marvin Sirbu, a CMU professor who heads the research of NetBill."[11]

Informedia technology has also been used to develop a virtual interview capability. Internet users can ask questions about products and services, explore Las Vegas tourist attractions, or ask sports stars about their game-winning strategies. The conversations employ voice recognition and semantic text analysis to provide answers to random questions from the "caller."

---

[10]This text was taken directly from Informedia's Web page at http://www.informedia.cs.cmu.edu/.

[11]Julian Neiser, "CyberCash Buys CMU Web Utility: Mellon to Help Test New System for Internet Cash Transactions," *Pittsburgh Business Times*, 1997.

These and other applications use Informedia to support knowledge management infrastructure and new applications that may change the way we think about business. Other commercial applications may include training or medical consultation.

Suggest a promising application for Informedia technology and use the evaluation framework to help decide how it should be structured to meet the knowledge management goals you have set for it. What are the most important constraints on the use of this new technology and will they be mitigated in the near future?

9

IMPLEMENTING KNOWLEDGE MANAGEMENT

Practical implementation of knowledge management initiatives will ultimately be based on the manager's point of view or framework. Those using the Industrial Age framework will aim to create a "well-oiled machine" with replaceable parts that behave according to mechanistic principles. Those using the Information Age framework will attempt to create an environment in which knowledge can be organically grown and harvested and see the challenge arising from a complex environment that is changing in largely unpredictable ways.

The second framework is a better match for creative knowledge management in the modern world of business. As a result, this chapter focuses exclusively on principles of implementation that can be explained within this framework. The guiding assumptions include:

- Self-organizing feedback based on the value and cost of units of knowledge is needed.
- Companies' knowledge asset portfolios and gaps therein must be assessed continuously.
- Creation of intellectual capital through tools and methodologies that encourage self-adaptive activities is essential.
- Algorithmically definable knowledge and creative knowledge must be distinguished.

Given that knowledge management within this framework is an emerging area, these assumptions represent a partial list.

Managers' roles within this framework involve nurturing, supporting, teaching, and providing meaningful performance feedback to the employees who are engaged in the tangible production of value. In addition, managers must decide how best to deploy knowledge among people and technology to earn the highest returns on that knowledge.

We build a case for a focus on companies core processes and view the companies as knowledge asset portfolios with gaps that must be filled to meet current and future management goals. We conclude with sample approaches to implementing knowledge management strategies.

"Electronic Propinquity"

In today's economy information and telecommunication systems are in the "electronic propinquity" (i.e., providing closeness or nearness electronically) business. Human behavior research shows that we not only typically "marry the girl/boy next door" but propinquity also affects how often we communicate with each other, how much we influence each other, and a host of other social impacts on relationships.

Electronic propinquity can serve as a surrogate for physical propinquity, and as such the information technology infrastructure plays a critical role in taking advantage of this important social phenomena.[1] Recognizing that knowledge is a critical corporate asset has produced the proliferation of tools to amplify the benefits of propinquity through creating, sharing, synthesizing, storing, accessing, and using knowledge. The promises of knowledge management are intertwined with information technology tools designed to support it.

All industries as well as their suppliers and customers stand to benefit from the new knowledge management framework for conducting business. Information technology industries can provide the tools and the infrastructure necessary to facilitate amplified electronic propinquity with customers. In addition, firms can learn from companies within and outside their industry borders.

Taken together these two benefits promise immense gains in knowledge creation, conversion of knowledge to value, and more effective knowledge reuse. Across whole industries, these gains enable better electronic linkages to speed product development, more rapidly meet market demands, reduce the cost of procurement, quickly set acceptable standards, and increase emphasis on creating new customer value. Customers benefit through improved relationships with suppliers, products customized specifically to meet their needs, and more personal time derived from electronic facilitation of their daily needs for services and products. The infrastructure that evolved to enable electronic propinquity also provides a technological foundation for the paradigm shift to knowledge management and its implementations.

Shifting the Paradigm

Shifting from the industrial paradigm to a knowledge management framework requires concrete steps that can easily be communicated to the entire workforce. Knowledge managers should look for early "base hits" and wait for "home runs" to come when critical mass has been built.

The initial focus should be on gaps between current assets and those needed to compete in the evolving marketplace. Core process operations touch everyone on a daily basis. Their well-being is essential because they produce the products and services that paying customers buy.

[1] See Larry Railing and Thomas J. Housel, *The Network Infrastructure to Contain Costs and Enable Fast Response: The TRW Process, MIS Quarterly,* 14, no. 4 (1990), pp. 405–19. This article describes how TRW's Space Park telecommunications network infrastructure allowed the rapid formation of project teams that were geographically distributed throughout the company without the necessity of collocating them physically, leading to faster response to new opportunities.

Knowledge Asset Portfolio

Creation and utilization of knowledge in core processes is the engine of wealth in the Information Age. Accelerating the conversion of knowledge into money is the real challenge in the Information Age, and the "knowledge payoff" occurs when knowledge is converted into bottom-line value in the form of a concrete, saleable product.

The learning-knowledge-value spiral depicted in Figure 9.1 assumes that the marketplace is the final arbiter of the value of knowledge when it speaks by buying a product or service, which is the result of the application of corporate knowledge. Customer purchasing decisions change the environment, and knowledge-based companies must respond by producing more highly valued products based on market feedback. This market feedback highlights needs for product changes and stimulates learning to acquire new knowledge to embed in processes that produce new products. The cycle then repeats itself with every market reaction. We view the transformation of learning into knowledge as a core activity that ultimately results in value embedded in processes that produce saleable products, and demonstrates a fundamental connection between learning, knowledge, and value.

The basic steps in implementing the knowledge management initiatives resulting from this connection can be characterized by managers' answers to the following questions.

1. What will the customer buy and why?
2. What core process knowledge is needed to produce the product?
3. What knowledge can be easily embedded in existing and/or new IT?
4. What is the improvement in return on that knowledge from embedding it in IT?
5. Should it be produced internally or outsourced?

FIGURE 9.1   Learning-Knowledge-Value Spiral

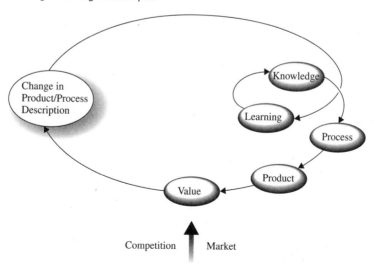

6. How long will it take to get the changed or new processes up to speed?
7. How soon will the entire cycle repeat itself?
8. How will our competition respond?

Tracking this conversion process in an objective way may become the foundation for accounting and finance in the digital economy. In this sense, effective knowledge management becomes a problem of how to deploy a portfolio of knowledge assets to create tangible value. This is a radical departure from Industrial Age–based accounting and finance in which tangible assets were viewed as the primary tools of value creation. It will require the abandonment of the comfortable categories of revenue and cost centers, since all processes create more or less value depending on the returns on knowledge they generate. The portfolio approach views corporations as internal marketplaces where core processes can be compared in terms of their returns on knowledge (ROK). To create a successful portfolio, managers must determine where the gaps are in their corporate knowledge assets.

Gaps in Knowledge Asset Portfolios

Knowledge gaps represent incomplete knowledge asset portfolios. These gaps surface in process failures that reduce the ROK of a company and are both current and future. Current gaps represent day-to-day process failures euphemized as "work arounds," rework, slow cycle times, errors, and so forth. Future gaps represent failure in management's ability to strategically determine what kinds of knowledge assets must be added or deleted to respond to a constantly changing marketplace and to take the necessary steps to ensure that they are deployed as required to meet the demands of that marketplace.

The promise of the Information Age has largely been based on the assumption that current employee knowledge could be redeployed within information systems and networks to reduce the cost of knowledge use within core processes. The Information Age has failed to deliver on this promise because:

1. Existing manual processes should have been reengineered before they were automated.
2. Knowledge better left in employees' heads has been redeployed in IT.
3. Cost-based process performance metrics designed to track performance for the Industrial Age remain in use.
4. Information technology has not been seen as a way to take advantage of future opportunities.
5. Artificial intelligence has failed to capture human decision-making capabilities.

Viewing corporations as portfolios of knowledge assets recognizes that the real problem is making sure that current and future knowledge gaps are properly managed. This new framework allows corporations to hold management accountable for the contributions of the knowledge assets and forces them to think more strategically about the knowledge assets they will need to capture new opportunities.

In addition, this approach will enhance cooperation among core process managers because they can now negotiate with each other and outsourcers to move knowledge assets to processes that generate the greatest returns. This differs from existing cost-based views of processes in which managers are rewarded for transferring their operating costs to others. This change is precipitated by the fact that knowledge assets are viewed as surrogates for value rather than solely as costs. Moreoever, managers can be held accountable for both cost and value.

As with any portfolio, investors, including both corporations and shareholders, expect a given level of return. Corporations are forced to invest in all the core processes required to produce their products, and even virtual corporations must invest in core processes whether they are outsourced or insourced. For this reason, more accurate metrics for "return" might include "cash-flow from core process," "return on knowledge," "return on process," or relative operating margins. External metrics would include earnings per share, operating margin, and cash-flow from operations. All such metrics must assess the successfulness of knowledge management implementations.

Designing Knowledge-Based Implementations[2]

Verna Allee has developed an implementation method to stimulate creative problem solving from a knowledge management perspective. She has used this method to design knowledge management solutions, and the following is taken from her recent work on value networks.

At the core of the enterprise, one will always find the traditional value chain operating in the core business process. However, in the knowledge economy, flow of goods and financial returns are increasingly only a part of the asset picture for overall company valuation. None of the value chain models capture important aspects and dynamics of a value network, such as:

The players: Business partners, important actors or influencers, and cocreators of products or services, including customers who may contribute value-generating activity or knowledge.

Dynamic value exchanges: Direct one-to-one value exchanges that happen between all the players in the extended enterprise.

Flow of intangible benefits: Flow of benefits gained in the form of intangible assets or benefits such as brand relationship, customer loyalty, extended capability, or strategic insight.

Knowledge exchanges: Exchanges of knowledge that support all business activity: strategic, tactical, and operational knowledge.

Transactions: Specific transactions and activities that generate value.

Products: Specific tangible and intangible products, or messages that are exchanged in the value network.

---

[2]The following section comes from Verna Allee's *Understanding the Value Network,* draft of article for publication, all rights reserved.

An Example of Value Exchange

Let's consider the three key value flows, or exchanges, in a value network and look at an example:

1. Goods, services, and revenue
2. Knowledge
3. Intangible benefits

One way to understand these flows is to focus on the dynamics of exchange. Whenever something happens, there is a response. Within the larger flows are numerous small events, which are called transactions or exchanges. Every exchange is supported by some mechanism or medium that enables the transaction, such as a technology.

The following example demonstrates these exchanges. Let's say as a technology provider that you would like to provide an online user group for your customers for a fee of $20 per month. The *mechanism* of an interactive user group allows several exchanges of value to take place between the provider and the user. Table 9.1 lists the value exchanges that might be enabled through such a mechanism.

1. The traditional value chain exchange is the provision of moderated discussions, information, and responses to questions in exchange for a fee.
2. The knowledge flow may involve exchanges of customer usage data and feedback for product development. As a result of their participation, the value-added knowledge that the user receives in exchange may be personally targeted news or offerings based on their unique personal preferences.
3. By tracing the intangible benefits that accrue in the network, one finds that the underlying logic for creating such a discussion group is not so much about gaining revenue from the service (indeed it may barely break even). The user group may really be about providing a sense of community on the part of the user. In return, of course, one would hope to receive an intangible benefit such as an increase in customer loyalty.

TABLE 9.1   EXAMPLE OF VALUE EXCHANGE

Mechanism	Provides user value	Returns value
Interactive On-Line Discussion Group	GOODS, SERVICE • Moderated discussions • Responses to questions	REVENUE • Subscription fee
	KNOWLEDGE • Personally targeted news, offerings based on user preferences	KNOWLEDGE • Feedback for product development • Customer usage data
	VALUE • Sense of community	VALUE • Customer loyalty

Using the same example we can "map" these value exchanges as a flow diagram showing services and revenue, knowledge flow, and intangible value creation. In this example the methodology employed is the *Holomapping^TM3* technique, a dynamic whole-system mapping methodology. See Figure 9.2.

An Example of a Value Network Diagram

Direct revenue value exchanges are but part of the picture in a value network. The flow of knowledge and intangible value is of equal importance. Figure 9.3 depicts the value exchanges that have been enabled by providing a marketing website to distributors. In this case, a manufacturer is providing distributor websites at their expense but have designed them so that competing manufacturers can sell products via the same website. Why in the world would a company provide a marketing capability to a competitor? In this example, the selling of competitor products on a manufacturer's website only makes sense by understanding the flow of *knowledge* and *intangible benefits* that are gained, such as competitive intelligence and market insight. The diagram provides a way to actually analyze and map the logic and resulting exchanges that take place. Only one type of exchange, that of goods, services, and revenue, has been part of traditional value-chain thinking. Now we must find ways to understand the other two types of exchanges as well.

These diagrams can be augmented with various types of documentation tables that detail each transaction or identify critical factors for each such as measures or dependencies.

FIGURE 9.2   Mapping the Exchanges

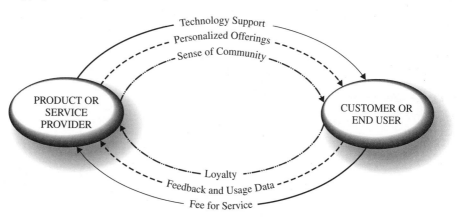

[3]Holomapping is a registered trademark of Verna Allee and Integral Performance Group.

FIGURE 9.3   Value Network Analysis Diagram

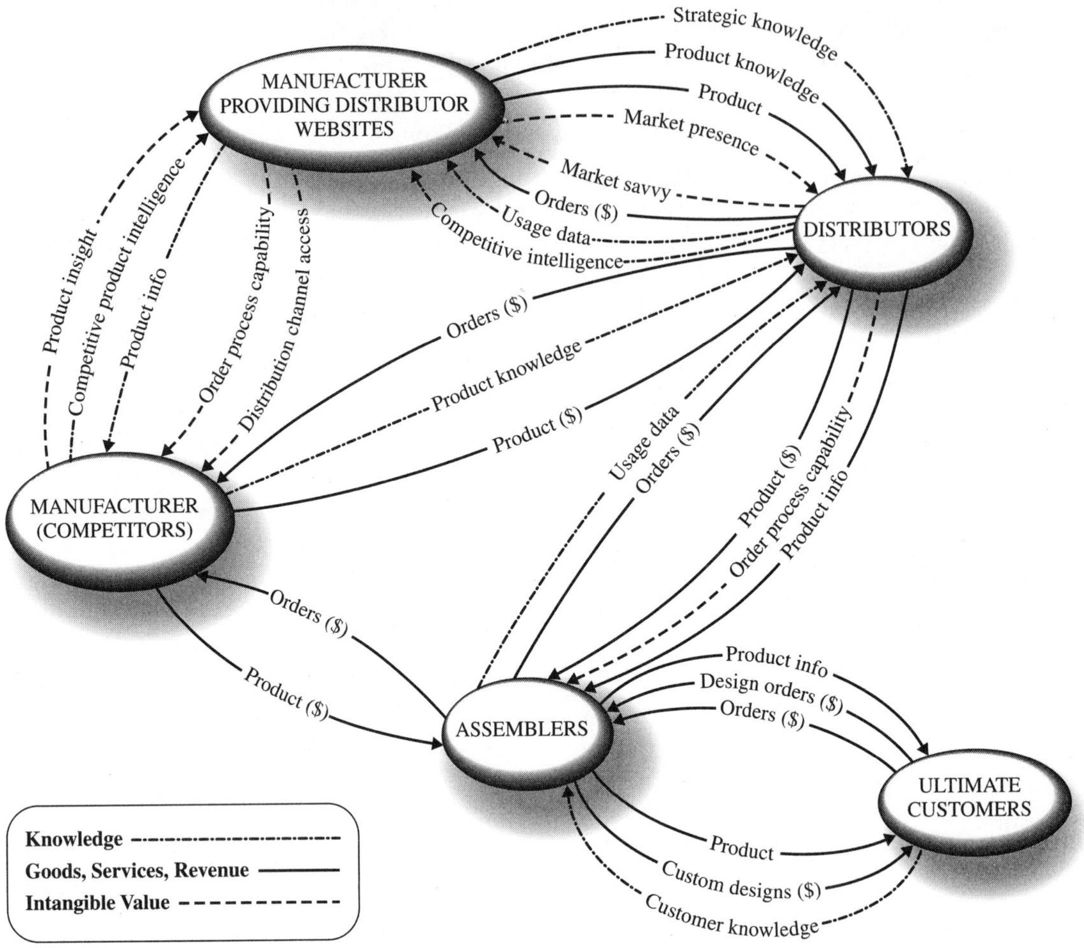

TO DEEPEN ANALYSIS

The Value Network Diagram serves as a systems map, containing a wealth of information, including:

- Boundaries of the system (what is included).
- Actors and entities (participants).
- All the mission-critical products in the system.
- Inputs and outputs.
- All key transactions and processes.
- Mission-critical knowledge exchanges.

- Intangible benefit gain.
- Sequences of events.
- Feedback loops.
- Exchanges or transactions and response.

Each exchange in the diagram can be sequenced, showing the order of each event or transaction. By creating a table depicting the time relationships, it is possible to reduce cycle time for the flows and optimize interactions across the whole system. The use of tables and matrixes linked with the value network diagram allows deeper analysis in a wide variety of arenas as well as versatility in application. This is a sampling of insights and applications that have been generated using a Value Network Analysis.

- Over two months' cycle time reduction for a product launch effort in a company of over 100,000 employees.
- Designing knowledge flow and exchanges for complex technology transfer.
- Reorganization of a multinational cross-functional services function for a large telecom.
- Design of delivery process and data capture for evaluation of training.
- Identification and analysis (including measures) of the three key value flows for a staff services function for a multinational high-tech company.
- Comparative analysis of electronic commerce value networks.
- Identifying venture capital partners and defining strategic relationships and business exchanges for a technology company start-up.
- Reducing software development time by generating a more tightly linked transaction-based enterprise model.

Value networks are complex. They encompass much more than the flow of products, services, and revenue of the traditional value chain. Whenever there is a transaction in a complex enterprise, there is an exchange of value. Yet, only a portion of value exchange can be tracked or measured through service delivery or revenue generation. As more and more products and services depend on the exchange of knowledge and information, knowledge becomes a medium of exchange in its own right. Astute management of knowledge exchanges can lead to solid gains in strategy development, improved operations, or enhanced image and brand identity.

Direct revenue exchanges are but part of the picture. As mediums of exchange, knowledge and intangible benefits are of equal importance. In the knowledge economy these may indeed tell much more about the present and future capability of the enterprise to achieve sustainable advantage. Particularly in the world of the Internet, these principles are being proven with unprecedented stock prices for companies such as Amazon.com booksellers and eBay, the online auction company. These companies, and others such as Cisco Systems, Dell Computers, and GE are gaining market valuation based not only on traditional financial measures but largely because of intangible assets that are accumulating from astute management of the value network.

Verna Allee's knowledge management implementation heuristic provides a very useful way to relatively quickly assess the value networks within a given company based on its knowledge assets. This heuristic is an important first step in developing an overall knowledge management strategy. A subsequent step might be to determine the level of maturity of a company's knowledge management efforts.

The Knowledge Management Maturity Model

The Knowledge Management Maturity (KMM) Model is used to assess the relative maturity of a company's knowledge management efforts. It was developed by Dr. V. P. Kochikar and his team at INFOSYS Technologies Incorporated. While it is a relatively new tool, it is well grounded in the capability maturity model derived from software development techniques.

The KMM model is used as an assessment tool to help focus and prioritize efforts to increase a business's current knowledge management maturity level. It assumes that all organizational learning is focused on delivering value to the customer, and encompasses an equally weighted three-pronged approach of managing knowledge within people, process, and technology.[4] An organization's KMM level can be at any of five different levels characterized by a "knowledge life cycle" that encompasses knowledge acquisition, dissemination, and reuse. The benefits of knowledge management implementation can be quantified at level four and higher. Level one is the default stage in which there is low commitment to managing anything other than essential, necessary survival-level tasks. At level one formal training is the main mechanism for learning, and all learning is taken to be reactive. Moreover, level-one organizations fragment knowledge into isolated pockets that are not explicitly documented.

Level-two organizations share only routine and procedural knowledge. Need-to-know is characteristic, and knowledge awareness rises with the realization that knowledge is an important organizational resource that must be managed explicitly. Senior management at level two recognizes the need for managing knowledge formally, and content-capturing processes become increasingly important. Databases and routine tasks exist but are not centrally compiled or managed. Knowledge of routine tasks is recorded and stored in a variety of diverse, rudimentary, and obsolete systems and formats that support only routine and procedural sharing. Online and technology-based learning mechanisms are in place but remain largely reactive.

Level-three organizations are aware of the need for managing knowledge. Content fit for use in all functions begins to be organized into a knowledge life cycle, and enterprise knowledge-propagation systems are in place. However, general awareness and maintenance are limited, and corporate expertise is applied in technologically complex, unfamiliar, or critical areas. Organizations at this level begin to collect and establish metrics for knowledge management and link knowledge management implementation with business results and productivity gains.

---

[4]This information about the KMM model was taken from a lecture by Dr. Kochikar to the University of Southern California Marshall School of Business on September 18, 2000.

Central knowledge organizations with people dedicated to overseeing the knowledge management infrastructure and content may be present but are not well defined. Core process knowledge is structured, categorized, and accessed, and it is somewhat integrated into existing information technology architecture. Access to knowledge is shared across the organization but is not fully integrated.

Enterprise knowledge sharing systems are characteristic of level four. These systems respond proactively to the environment and the quality, currency, utility, and usage of these systems is improved. Knowledge processes are scaled up across the organization, and organization knowledge boundaries become blurred. Benefits of knowledge sharing and reuse can be explicitly quantified, and training moves to an ad hoc basis as the technology infrastructure for knowledge sharing is increasingly integrated and seamless. Content is enlivened as experts across the organization contribute liberally to the system and knowledge life cycle processes are mapped. Most importantly, content is managed, created, shared, and reused as the benefits of knowledge sharing are quantified.

At level five, knowledge sharing is institutionalized and organizational boundaries are minimized. Human know-how and content expertise are integrated into a seamless package, and knowledge can be most effectively leveraged. Level-five organizations have the ability to accelerate the knowledge life cycle to achieve business advantage.

The Knowledge Management Maturity Model promises to focus and prioritize knowledge management implementation. Sustainable bottom-line benefits are evident, but this approach is new and requires further testing and refinement. More specific knowledge management implementations that are in the process of being refined are customer relationship management and supply chain management.

Managing Customer Relationship and Supply Chain Knowledge

Knowledge management can be fruitfully applied to e-customer relationship management (eCRM) and supply chain management. Both employ basic guidelines for knowledge management implementation.

Many electronic commerce retailers have failed because they overlooked the requirements of managing large physical inventories. Unable to fulfill customer orders and deliver their goods as promised, e-tailers suffered from customer backlash, and as a consequence, order fulfillment and inventory logistics have become very important.

Inventory caching prevents fulfillment failures but is incredibly costly. Strategic partnerships with suppliers and inventory logistic companies is a better solution. Figure 9.4 illustrates potential problems in supply chain management, and Figure 9.5 illustrates a successful fulfillment system. Many problems are caused by assuming that orders passed along to manufacturers will be successfully filled. Moreover, e-tailers rely on suppliers' inventories and ability to ship directly to customers. Also, packing and shipping for home delivery is a very labor-intensive process. Even e-tailers that are good at personalizing their Web interfaces for individual customers may fail when they try to reproduce the equivalent of L.L. Bean's physical inventory management system.

Many companies are ready to ship hundreds or thousands of items to a single destination, but they are often not prepared to gift-wrap and ship products for home delivery.

FIGURE 9.4   The Supply Chain

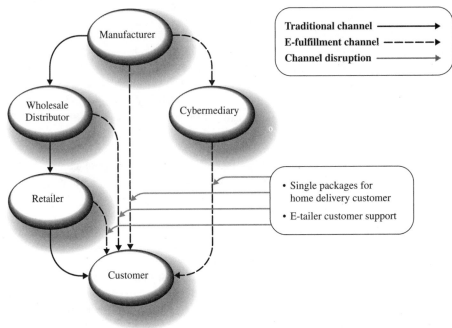

Source: UPS Logistics.

FIGURE 9.5   Order Fulfillment System

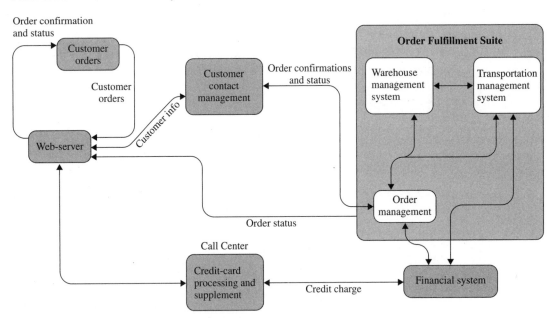

FIGURE 9.6   Generic CRM Model[9]

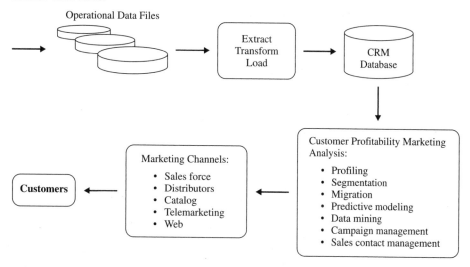

In addition, customers may believe displayed items are in stock, but this is not necessarily true. E-tailers must realize that managing their customer relationships also requires control of their supply chains.

Successfully managing supply chain knowledge is a key to managing customer relationships and fulfillment systems. Figure 9.5 has many advantages over the model in Figure 9.4: It incorporates additional features, including work-flow management and alliances with strategic partners. Efficient communication leads to faster order processing and fulfillment throughout the system. In addition, order management encompasses both transportation systems and warehouse management. Warehouse management must track inventory and relay this information to customers. This also requires a scalable means of packing and shipping for home delivery.[5]

A third key feature is customer relationship management. As important as warehousing and transportation management, is customer relationships involve profiling and analyzing trends from databases. Finally, effective management of finance systems involves credit-card processing and authorization procedures, payment collection, and reducing fraudulent purchases to speed the order-fulfillment process.

Managing supply chain knowledge can produce benefits beyond the e-tailing market space. Supply chain management is an important element of any knowledge management implementation plan for companies that rely on outside partners. Figure 9.5 displays just one approach to managing supply chain knowledge but serves as a template that can be adapted to the particular needs of a company.

Just as supply chain management requires knowledge about corporate partners, eCRM systems offer new opportunities to understand and bond with customers (see Figure 9.6—Generic CRM Model). Development of the Internet has created a new

[5]Jerry Kurtyka, *Knowledge Management* (December 1999), p. 85.

marketing channel, since consumers are now available and easy to contact electronically, but customer loyalty is not assured because competing options are a click away.[6]

Marketers and salespeople are no longer able to make that "personal connection with a customer that really solidifies a relationship. On the other hand, e-commerce opens up some great possibilities for getting to know your customers in ways that were previously impossible."[7] Ultimately, capturing and acting upon knowledge about customers enhances the possibility of positive customer responses by delivering "a consistent marketing message across all channels and customer touchpoints."[8] Business's knowledge of customers through multichannel response capabilities increases marketing and economic performance.

In closed-loop CRM systems, customer "regularities" are recorded, stored, and analyzed. These regularities allow marketers to analyze patterns in historical customer data and predict future customer behaviors. Marketers can target potentially responsive customers.

> This implies that it is possible for the marketer to exercise a degree of control over the customer relationship because the customer's response is, to some degree, predictable. However, this control becomes questionable when the customer has many competing alternatives for their attention and pocketbook. That is what is meant by the term "open market." The marketing loop is "closed" only in respect to the customers' relationship with the business, but consumers exist in an open web of many buying relationships.[10]

Kurtyka offers a practical eCRM approach to managing customer knowledge. The "Circle of Life" approach (see Figure 9.7) displays a knowledge management implementation heuristic in the eCRM context.[11]

The four steps are described in detail below.

1. Precampaign research and analysis
   A. Through a prior analysis of market segmentation and propensity modeling, customers and prospects are selected and placed on a target list. In this step, customers who do not wish to be contacted should be removed from the target list.
   B. Determine what will be targeted to each of the different customer groups.
2. Campaign initiatives
   A. Design the marketing campaign to effectively use the various combinations of channels (e.g., direct mail, call center, e-mail, point-of-purchase).
3. The physical campaign
   A. Release the target list through the various marketing channels.
4. Postcampaign analysis
   A. Evaluate and analyze the marketing campaign results from the responses.
   B. Adjust the marketing campaign in response to the analysis.

---

[6]Ibid.
[7]Ibid.
[8]Ibid.
[9]Ibid., p. 86.
[10]Ibid., p. 85.
[11]Ibid.

FIGURE 9.7   Marketing "Circle of Life"

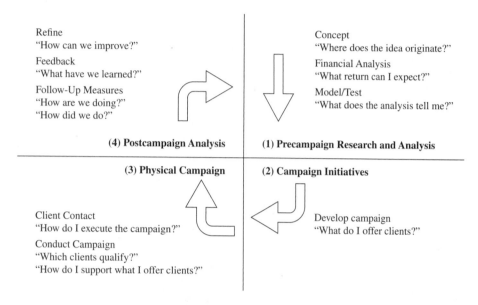

Refine
"How can we improve?"

Feedback
"What have we learned?"

Follow-Up Measures
"How are we doing?"
"How did we do?"

Concept
"Where does the idea originate?"

Financial Analysis
"What return can I expect?"

Model/Test
"What does the analysis tell me?"

(4) Postcampaign Analysis

(1) Precampaign Research and Analysis

(3) Physical Campaign

(2) Campaign Initiatives

Client Contact
"How do I execute the campaign?"

Conduct Campaign
"Which clients qualify?"
"How do I support what I offer clients?"

Develop campaign
"What do I offer clients?"

C. Through collecting customer responses and placing them into a CRM database, businesses can track the effectiveness of their campaigns. They then can use this customer data to refine future campaigns.

Collecting and managing customer knowledge through eCRM allows businesses to capture and act upon customer propensities. It increases marketing effectiveness by delivering consistent messages through multiple channels including flyers, television and print advertisements, and Internet banners or pop-ups. The four-stage approach recognizes the realities of a Web-connected customer base and helps knowledge management teams implement more effective customer knowledge management programs.

CONCLUSION

Company management cannot be timid in developing and implementing new approaches to managing knowledge. The new paradigm marks a discontinuous shift in fundamental assumptions and requires new frameworks for implementation of management strategies.

Verna Allee's value networks heuristic provides one very promising approach for developing effective corporate level knowledge strategies. The KMM maturity model will help organizations determine how sophisticated their current knowledge management efforts are and provide guideposts for tracking their progress. Supply chain and eCRM techniques offer some relatively concrete steps for implementing knowledge management strategies.

Knowledge management efforts should begin with assessment of knowledge portfolios and end with concrete steps to fill current and future needs. Methods for filling these knowledge needs must be based on improvements in returns on knowledge that they will generate. Creating a learning-knowledge-value cycle that spirals toward greater and greater market value is the ultimate goal.

QUESTIONS FOR REVIEW

1. What are the guiding principles underlying any knowledge management implementation strategy? Did the chapter miss any important ones?
2. What does the current state of knowledge management have to do with developing an effective implementation strategy?
3. What will it take to create an effective use of the principle of electronic propinquity?
4. How do the knowledge gap assessment and the value exchange networks method create a common reference for planning a knowledge management implementation effort?
5. How can company knowledge management executives use the KMM model to assess their company's readiness for new knowledge management strategies?
6. How should companies include supply chain knowledge in their knowledge management strategies?
7. What benefits do eCRM methods offer for e-commerce companies as well as traditional retailers? How should they include this capability in managing customer knowledge?
8. What are the largest impediments to making a knowledge management strategy really work?

EXERCISE: Develop a Knowledge Strategy

Select a traditional retailer and an e-tailer. Develop a knowledge management strategy for each along with a knowledge management implementation plan based on the principles and tools discussed in this chapter. For example, you might look at Sears and eToys or Home Depot and Amazon.com. Be sure to consider the supply chain and eCRM models.

You will need to gather information about each company from traditional sources, including the popular press, stock analysis, company 10Ks, and annual reports. You may also visit physical outlets and websites. You may even conduct telephone and/or face-to-face interviews with company executives.

Start by evaluating their current operations and any knowledge management problems they appear to have. Then, project what knowledge they will need to succeed in the future and identify any gaps in their knowledge asset portfolios. Try to estimate how your knowledge management strategy will affect their return on knowledge.

You might even share your work with the executives that you have interviewed to solicit feedback on your plan.[12]

[12]Coincidentally, three of the MBAs in my spring 2000 knowledge management class received excellent job offers as a result of completing this exercise and feeding the results back to company executives.

10

THE FUTURE OF KNOWLEDGE MANAGEMENT

As the previous chapters have suggested, the future of knowledge management is impacted by new chip technologies that make the storage, organization, retrieval, application, and measurement of knowledge easier than ever before. But while these technological options can help us imagine new horizons for knowledge measurement and management, they are not in themselves the force or substance of imagination. Looking even a few years into the future requires a leap of thinking—almost a leap of faith—that takes us beyond the capabilities of current or projected technologies. As thinkers from Plato to Einstein have argued, "The poets get there first." That is, the imaginative leap that cannot be substantiated at present often proves, like lightning, to be the flash of insight we need to drive the technologies of knowledge management toward useful human goals.

This exploration of the future of knowledge management is therefore imbued with poetry and vision—defiantly so. We begin with a paradox: At the same time that *knowledge seeking* has never been more intense, widely distributed, and generally successful, the experience of "having knowledge" and managing it is becoming less common for the vast majority of us.

Put another way, more research is occurring in virtually all fields than ever before, with an astounding total output of new knowledge. One could expect "knowledge management" to involve little more than a good storage system for all these knowledge items. Fortunately, the future seems to hold more in store for us than a better filing cabinet.

In an era of knowledge explosion, the experience of the average man or woman, or for that matter, the researcher in his or her private life, is one of knowledge evaporation or, more accurately, knowledge sequestration. "Someone somewhere knows," we tell ourselves when dealing with telecommunications, medicine, household appliances, the symbols of religion, and so forth—but that "someone" is distinctly not us. We are becoming increasingly comfortable inhabiting a dense fog in which switches click, devices whirr, chemicals fizz, things happen, but for the life of us we can't say how or why. We are becoming comfortable as knowledge-less people, which, as we shall see, is quite different from being ignorant people.

THE ERA OF EMBEDDED KNOWLEDGE

With such proliferation of knowledge, what has happened to our experience of "knowing things"? What happened to accessible knowledge? To knowing what made things tick? In a word, much knowledge has become *embedded*.

Take a simple example of knowledge embedding. Sally, a five-year-old, has the misfortune of having two older brothers who will not rest until they teach her how to ride a bicycle. They begin by dispensing knowledge in its old-fashioned, accessible form (available, in other words, to anyone who speaks the language in which the knowledge is framed). Among their pearls of wisdom are the following points:

"These are the handlebars."
"These are the pedals."
"Don't go too slow or lean over. You'll fall over."
"Don't turn the handlebars too far. You'll fall over."
"Keep pedaling or you'll fall over."
"Don't stand up on the pedals. You'll fall over."
"When you put on your brakes to stop, stick your foot out or you'll fall over."
"Don't go off the curb. You'll fall over."

At this point, knowledge is unembedded. It can be discussed, debated, repeated over and over by Sally, even written down into a book on bicycling or scripted as a television show. But mark the transformation that takes place as Sally learns to actually ride her bicycle. During a few shaky tours around the block, she manages to *embed* knowledge—her brothers' lessons become "part of her," but are no longer accessible as discrete items of knowledge. She quits saying to herself, "Keep pedaling, don't lean over!" (unembedded knowledge). Once adept at bike-riding, she no longer stops to think about specific rubrics for when or how fast to pedal, particular names for the parts of the bicycle, or other items of bike-riding knowledge that seemed of paramount importance during her first wobbly attempts. In short, the knowledge involved in bike riding has become second nature for Sally.

The price, of course, of acquiring embedded, "second nature" knowledge is the loss of what we can call "first nature" or unembedded knowledge. In matters ranging from tying a tie or shoelace to holding a puppy or swimming underwater, we quickly reach a point where we "no longer stop to think about it"—and literally have difficulty reclaiming the first knowledge we require to teach someone else to do it.

In frustration, we resort to demonstration: "Here, let me show you how to do it. I can't explain it." But *showing*, however effective in some circumstances, subverts *telling*. Embedded knowledge ultimately prefigures a world in which knowledge is beyond language—in which you "have to see it to believe it." And what if you want to understand? "You had to be there" may be the sad mantra not just of aging hippies but serious teachers as well who strive to deal with a world of embedded knowledge.

OMNIPRESENT EMBEDDING

Extrapolate from these simple examples a world in which *most* important knowledge exists only in embedded form. Imagine that the cell phone in your pocket is a virtual mystery to you. Dependent though you are on it, you have only the vaguest notions of how it connects you to a business associate in Hong Kong. "Satellite," you may tell yourself, but that word (like the term "cell phone") is more a gesture than an explanation—a mystery wrapped in an enigma.

Imagine, further, that the pill you take to combat depression, hypertension, allergies, or another malady is no less a mystery to you. You depend on it, but you have no idea how it works. For that matter, your prescribing physician is only dimly aware of its underlying electrochemical effects in the mind/body, and surely has no time to share these small bits of knowledge with you. Like the pill, the physician is a form of embedded knowledge that usually cannot be called back to an accessible level.

Or contemplate the airline on which you pile up your frequent-flyer miles. You know how to get on and off, but you have no meaningful knowledge of what holds the tons of metal in the air. "Jet engines," you tell yourself, in effect pasting a superficial label on the knowledge package that remains opaque and mysterious. The same general exercise could be undertaken for shampoo, computers, television, microwave ovens, glue, and all the rest of modern life's gems of embedded knowledge.

At the same time that massive stores of knowledge went into the making of each of these marvels, those stores of knowledge are locked for most of us. Like riding a bicycle, we *use* them without wanting or needing to *know* them.

The idea of "locked knowledge" is not intended as conspiratorial. Except for the zealous efforts of companies to protect their intellectual property, few of the core ideas of our era are inaccessible to the public—even more so in the Internet Age. General Electric does not prevent you from learning at any public library or Internet encyclopedia site what makes a microwave oven burn your popcorn.

But you won't study microwaves tonight, nor will the authors of this book. Although no one prohibits us from reclaiming unembedded knowledge, we have learned to content ourselves with "second nature" knowledge for an increasing number of the things, technological and otherwise, that we use as part of our living. Like Sally on her bike, we no longer "stop to think" about such things.

THE "KNOWING" RELATIONSHIP

Put another way, we will have less and less of a traditional "knowing" relationship in the years ahead with the things that surround us. If you have forgotten what it means and feels like to be in a "knowing" relationship with one's environment, recall your elementary school, high school, and college days, all of which were ostensibly dedicated to fostering this "knowing" relationship. Instead of simply knowing (like the first colonial farmers) that manure increases crop yield, you delved into the knowing relationship of root structures, osmosis, chlorophyll processes, nitrogen uptake, and so forth. The colonists knew only "manure," but you knew the underlying processes, at least in simplified form.

Instead of knowing (like the first automobile drivers) that the car had the power of a horse, you understood horsepower in terms of internal combustion and torque. Their paradigm or model for understanding was the plowhorse; yours was the controlled power of combustion.

Instead of simply knowing that, well, shit happens, you studied the purported causes of world wars. The paradigm for social upheaval of earlier ages was the unpredictability of fate or the displeasure of the gods; your paradigm was the predictability of social forces such as poverty, nationalism, and ego-crazed leadership.

All of this school-days knowledge was relatively unembedded. Teachers feared, in fact, the introduction into the classroom of the slide rule at first, then the calculator, spell-check programs, and the like for just this reason: Knowledge that could be held in unembedded form by students would now and forever be embedded inaccessibly in a device. The student could get the results faster but couldn't access the process leading to the results.

To teachers' relief, in biology or human physiology studies, no Star Trek tricorder gave complete readouts of life conditions. Students dissecting a frog or combining chemicals felt a connection between processes they observed and the knowledge by which they interpreted those processes. They valued the "Aha!" response as testimony to this connection (as compared to the "Ah!" response that testifies to the successful functioning of devices we don't understand).

CHOICES: UNEMBEDDED OR EMBEDDED KNOWLEDGE

But so what? Why should unembedded knowledge or embedded knowledge matter to us so long as technicians somewhere at Cisco Systems keep producing routers that successfully (and mysteriously) allows us to use the Web and engineers somewhere at Boeing keep behemoths at 30,000 feet?

Is there any advantage to acquiring even elementary knowledge of common technologies and processes—in effect, to keep some knowledge unembedded? Do I want or need to understand my toaster?

To address that question, return for a moment to Sally and the bike-riding scenario. We find her now in her college years applying for part-time work as a bike delivery person for an urban express messenger service. She trusts that the bike-riding knowledge that she has embedded, her "second nature" ability, will serve her well.

She's dead wrong, of course. Stick out a foot when you stop? Not unless you want to lose it in traffic. Avoid hopping off curbs? It's a requirement in the bike messenger business. Sit down on the bicycle seat? Hardly ever.

Put another way, Sally can't adjust successfully to the very changes she desires (money for college!) because she's stuck with an embedded knowledge paradigm that doesn't meet her needs as a would-be bike messenger. One disadvantage, then, of relying on "second nature" or embedded patterns of knowledge is that we *can't act* in our interest when circumstances change. We trust habit and have no recourse beyond habit. Collegiate and professional sports coaches face this impasse when they spend inordinate time and energy getting their athletes to break old, bad techniques (i.e., embedded knowledge paradigms), whether in the case of a runner with an ineffective stride, a swimmer with an uncoordinated breathing sequence, or a pitcher or passer with a tendon-tearing delivery. "I wish they had never learned in the first place," one coach complained. "Then I could teach them."

But can't Sally simply learn new ways to ride a bike to succeed as a messenger? Not as long as she defines bike riding in the terms and by the rules set down by her brothers long ago. A second disadvantage, then, of relying on embedded knowledge is that we *can't think* in our interest when circumstances change. Our categories of consciousness are limited by our embedded knowledge paradigms. We literally cannot see what's new because we insist upon viewing it through the dulling screen of what's old. Galileo faced excommunication over his assertion of a heliocentric planetary system not because his bishop knew *too little* to follow Galileo's evidence and argument but because the bishop knew *too much* of the Earth-centered paradigm, with all it implied of man's relation to God.

THE BIRTH AND DEATH OF PARADIGMS

Many companies have gone through excruciating growing pains—some of them fatal—because they cannot think beyond yesterday's paradigm. For decades, Nordstrom defined itself as an upscale clothier, a paradigm that enforced focus on acquiring sophisticated, well-made clothing, displaying it tastefully, and pricing it shrewdly. Nordstrom learned through increasing competition and falling profits in the 1980s that its embedded "clothier" paradigm kept the company from seeing its true future and self-interest.

As right as the paradigm seemed looking backward, it was all wrong looking forward. The company's highly successful current paradigm is as a "customer service and satisfaction" company, with all other priorities subordinated as supporting cast to this star ensemble of retail knowledge. The jury is still out on whether Sears, J. C. Penney, and other traditional retailers can see beyond the confines of their old merchandising paradigms to compete successfully in the Internet Age.

There is a certain Darwinism at work in the inevitable expiration of inadequate paradigms. At the corporate level, lousy paradigms bring eventual bankruptcy, while successful, adaptive paradigms yield increasing growth and profit. At the human level, the rather complete wiping out of the *Homo sapiens* population every 80 years or so makes room for new patterns of knowledge and experience. Like miniature corporations, each of us inevitably embeds knowledge and belief patterns that we are more than happy to foist upon our offspring, often without unembedded explanation.

Mercifully, the knowledge paradigms embedded in each of us typically share our mortality, with Victorianism dying with the last Victorian, and so forth. Freud's insistence that we are obsessed with killing our fathers probably has more to do with stale, boring paradigms than latent sexual strife.

But some of our knowledge paradigms are perpetuated beyond our human years. Traditionally, books (and in our time, films and computer storage) have been a central channel for, as Browning wrote, "lending our minds out" beyond their mortal limits. Music and the arts in all forms have similarly been a transgenerational repository for emotion, aesthetic response, and vision. Mozart, da Vinci, and company still live, at least in the context they valued most.

Institutions including the church in all its permutations have perpetuated knowledge paradigms largely unchanged across centuries. Sometimes the success of this embalming can be startling, as when items of knowledge intellectually and culturally meaningful in a former era such as the Virgin birth or eating the body and drinking the blood of Christ in communion come down to the Modern Age as quaint items of belief verging on the weird.

Government perpetuates knowledge paradigms to the extent it clings to constitutions, core concepts ("freedom," "democracy"), and shrines of events and heroes ("the spirit of Gettysburg"). Often these paradigms are mere rhetorical shams, dragged out for propagandistic purposes. One recalls Samuel Johnson's definition of "patriotism" as "the last refuge of a coward."

TECHNOLOGY AND EMBEDDED KNOWLEDGE

But as influential as all such forces have been, for better or worse, in freeing us for peaceful coexistence or condemning us to conflict, no force is more powerful for the future in perpetuating our central knowledge paradigms than the embedding functions of technology in all its forms.

The human race has had only a few hundred years' experience with the embedding power of widespread technology. Previously we as a race tried to use Nature as the primary vehicle for embedding our knowledge and belief. (By Nature, we include the whole tapestry, ranging from Yellowstone Park to clouds in the sky to the bird outside your window.)

Our efforts to embed knowledge into Nature had mixed success at best. As might be expected, sun worship in Egypt to banish storms had no better a track record than human sacrifice among the Incas to bring rain. Our nascent astrological sign proved powerless to ameliorate our day-to-day pain or long-term destiny, except perhaps in striking up conversation over drinks.

Nature was so obtuse as a vehicle for embedded human knowledge and belief that, for the Modern Age, it has become positioned as the great enemy of paradigm making—that "Other" reality that seemingly will not be contained within our limiting mental constructs. Nature (at least as we contemplate it) defies our efforts to make it a message bearer from generation to generation.

For most of us, the blue sky or distant mountains do not "mean" anything (i.e., carry embedded knowledge messages), although they may arouse certain highly individual feelings. The rainbow does not promise good fortune, nor does a particular configuration of stars or planets prefigure misfortune. Nature refuses to be had, in spite of our best efforts to bend it to our use.

A visit to any art gallery reveals ingenious attempts to make Nature speak a human message. In fact, whenever visual artists have been too successful at making Nature the message bearer of their era ("O beautiful, for spacious skies," etc.), the next generation of artists—Picasso and his followers, for example—visually smash the prevailing view of Nature and insist upon its independence or even hostility to human messages (which, of course, becomes its own paradigm to be destroyed by other generations of artists).

BEYOND NATURE: THE EMBEDDED ENVIRONMENT

But contemplate a world without Nature's stubbornness and vagaries, an environment in which applied and embedded knowledge has been harnessed to give us what we want. Imagine an external world in which stimuli for sensations and impressions are carefully controlled. We refer to omnipresent technologies for temperature control, air quality, light variation, sound optimization, ergonomics in all forms, and so forth.

That vision may be right at hand. For example, you move from your air-conditioned home to your air-conditioned BMW with its Bose CD system to your air-conditioned office wearing light-polarizing sunglasses and faux-silk undies in a generally rosy mood supported by your Prozac. That's a good start at a thoroughly embedded environment. Hundreds of thousands of discrete knowledge items, virtually all beyond your reach, contribute to the embedded technologies that you enjoy.

Add to that not-inconceivable vision the additional influence of internal technological controls, including physical and emotional medications, a variety of prostheses to repair or improve upon Nature (hearing aids, breast implants, and erectile pumps at present, with brain-interfacing memory chips, mechanical hearts, and other wonders to come), sensory stimulation and mediation in the form of virtual reality devices, and intellectual support for data gathering and decision making in the form of artificial intelligence mechanisms. The result is a technological forest where the individual twigs of knowledge are obscured almost entirely.

LIVING IN THE TECHNOLOGICAL FOREST

At the beginning of a new millennium, it's not difficult to imagine inhabiting such a technological forest. Most of us have at least one foot already firmly planted in such a world. In fact, we're not imagining at all here, but are simply calling to mind inventions and technological applications already on the market in one form or another. Truly imagining our lives a century from now may well involve a disconnect as dramatic as a caveman imagining IBM.

These changes will come. Our future comfort, pleasure, sense of security, aspirations for wealth and progress, and concern for the welfare of others all conspire to grow this technological forest. Within a generation we may well have thoroughly surrounded ourselves with techno-Nature that old-fashioned Nature may seem a distant, medieval dream.

We leave Nature because it will not obey and please us. The virtual reality version of tennis will be more fulfilling than whacking the actual ball on a skin-your-knee, high-humidity court. The visually and sensually mediated experience of the mountains or seashore through artificial means will be incomparably beautiful compared to the former "real" thing, thorns, jellyfish, and all. Sex without technological enhancements will be unpopular, then unthinkable. Business decision making without artificial intelligence (AI) support, then AI management will be foolhardy. Medical recommendations, then medical decisions for oneself and others will be made by computer and carried out artificially to avoid error. Chemical and noninvasive electronic therapies, including reparative MRI, will be fine-tuned to address the body's various complaints and potentials, including those of the mind.

The key point for our purposes is that in this brave new world not far off virtually all important knowledge will be completely embedded in the technologies that surround us (or around which we assemble, depending on your point of view). In the words of Arthur C. Clarke, "Any sufficiently advanced technology is indistinguishable from magic." In this world of magic, you won't know how the trick is played, nor will you often be conscious of when it is being played. The "magic" will be an expected part of the ordinary fabric of your existence.

FREEDOM AND META-KNOWLEDGE

Far from perceiving ourselves as captives of our embedded technologies in an era beyond Nature, we will probably feel that, more than ever, we are captains of our fates. We will be able to act quickly, if somewhat blindly, to address our problems and achieve our goals. We will have the general assurance that somewhere "out there" is a packaged solution to most of life's dilemmas. We won't know much in the traditional sense, but we will know a great deal about where to get what we need.

Our freedom, in short, will consist in our ability not to manage items of knowledge—that illusion passed with the 1990s and will seem quaint within a decade—but instead to manage meta-knowledge. Like shoppers for vacations, our professional and personal lives will be largely spent in search of conducive and affordable "packages" that achieve certain desirable effects. To the best of our abilities, we will select, install, and make decisions about the effectiveness of these packages. We will manage meta-knowledge.

The process is not unlike that we now employ with software. For example, few of us write our own code for accounting software. Instead, we read or hear about, then purchase software that may serve our needs (or, more accurately, may be served by our needs as we adjust our business processes to fit the preset parameters of the software). In this case, accounting software is meta-knowledge—deeply embedded items of specific mathematical knowledge wrapped in one seamless package that cannot be usefully disassembled. We do not inquire into its embedded knowledge any more than a cowboy frets about the molecular composition of his cows. In both cases, what matters are macro issues: round 'em up, roll 'em out, rawhide.

As managers of meta-knowledge, we will have little time or patience to alter the "item knowledge" content of the knowledge packages we decide to use. In fact, there will probably be more useful knowledge discarded in the coming decades than at any other time in human history, as software and other technology packages are trashed entirely because of a slight knowledge glitch or omission involving less than a fraction of 1 percent of the total knowledge package. In this way we will be imitating the spirit and practice of the Indy 500 race car owner who in the heat of the race changes out an entire engine or transmission rather than localizing and resolving small problems. Meta-knowledge managers are generally not interested in why packages fail. The decision is binary logic: It doesn't work, ergo replace it.

Special skills will be required for managers who spend their lives seeking, installing, uninstalling, and replacing packages of embedded knowledge, the deep workings of which they do not begin to grasp. Our white-collar education in the near future will consist primarily of acquainting us with the latest features of meta-knowledge packages for professional and personal use, just as a modern physician's education is now spent reviewing the pros and cons of the most potent pharmacology for various ills (as opposed to studying the underlying electrochemical processes of specific drug interaction in the body).

THE AGE OF META-KNOWLEDGE MANAGEMENT

Let us conclude by speculating about three implications of the Age of Meta-Knowledge Management. First, with considerable irony, it is entirely possible that this new age emerging from exercise of empiricism and rationality will end up being similar in its principal characteristics to the medieval Age of Faith. Unaware of their history or internal composition, we will cling to icons (including those on our computer-screen desktops) and saints ("Microsoft," "Apple," "Sun," etc.) with the same mixture of hope, devotion, and disgust as any of Chaucer's Canterbury pilgrims or sun worshippers of the past. We will believe, without proof and against experience, that the Creator(s) of our meta-knowledge packages would not sneak cookies onto our hard-drives without our permission, insert hidden tracking codes into our CPUs, or process our personal profile and purchasing information in such a way as to make us prey to unscrupulous and annoying marketeers.

In short, we will take our packages of meta-knowledge largely on faith. When our faith is shaken occasionally, we will rebel by leaving one branch and joining another within the one techno-church, perhaps by installing a new word-processing program or subscribing to a different Internet provider. In any case, we will expect to experience magic (i.e., results we expect but cannot account for), to be gratified by it, and to understand not a bit or byte of it. (Interestingly, we will be so unaware of its embedded knowledge that within an hour or two we will boast that we "understand" the new program thoroughly, without even working through the tutorial. One can imagine a Druid priest at Stonehenge surveying the night sky and making a similar claim for all-embracing understanding of the stars.)

Second, we as managers of meta-knowledge in a deeply embedded technical world will proceed by Continuous Improvement rather than by Quantum Leaps. The interconnected and interdependent nature of the various locked-in technologies within our professional and personal lives will make dramatic changes intellectually possible but practically undesirable, in the same way that the electric car has been locked out of mainstream development and capitalization by the interlocking web of oil-based autos and industries. So we will chip away, software release by release, at steady improvements in processing speed, software features, compatibility, and so forth rather than expecting or welcoming a paradigm-altering revolution.

Again, with considerable irony, the age most capable of making quantum leaps may prove to be the age least willing to do so.

Finally, our inexorable efforts to embed human knowledge in an external, technological environment will culminate in our eventual ability to embed ourselves—that is, to "download" all that we perceive as our unique consciousness to a host less vulnerable to the ravages of time and mortality.

This notion may not seem preposterous even to those most allegiant to existing paradigms. Devices now interface successfully with retinal nerves, auditory nerves, pancreatic and kidney functions, and, increasingly, brain functions associated with seizures, narcolepsy, and other ills. Alpha waves have been happily tapped to monitor and even create the "relaxation response." Given simultaneous and exponential progress in brain research and computer memory and processing power, it is no longer inconceivable that the mind can at some point be mapped and "read" for its electrochemical patterns of interaction. From that point on, we can well expect consciousness to be "born" externally.

It may feel odd in the extreme to contemplate ourselves as "programs" running in a supercomputer. Our first thoughts probably turn to what is lost—the sense of one's physical self, our pleasure in sensual contact of all kinds, and so forth. Those sensations, of course, can easily be taken along. If you miss your toes, certainly a program of the future can be tweaked a bit to give you virtual toes to your heart's delight, as real in your sensations as you now experience them or remodeled to excise bunions. (A well-supported discussion of the technological prospects for externalizing the human mind appears in Ray Kurzweil's *The Age of the Spiritual Machine: When Computers Exceed Human Intelligence* [Viking, 1999].)

We as sentient minds are each interfaced to our physical bodies and the external world by electrochemical signals not entirely unlike those passing through computers. The nature of those signals, not the physical realities to which they are linked, create our sensations. If the signals themselves can be accurately "faked," that is, stimulated without bondage or links to external realities like full stomachs and sunny days, we will not know the difference. "Is it real or is it virtual?" will become a moot question—what's real is what is sensed, whether from natural or artificial connections.

Certainly the vectors of human endeavor point toward this ultimate embedding of self. In frustration over the limitations of his hands, man invented external tools. In frustration over the limitations of his feet, man invented external transportation devices in all their forms. In frustration over the limitations of his eyes and ears, man invented external telephone, television, radio, motion pictures, and the rest. In frustration over the limitations of his emotional repertoire, man invented external stimuli in the form of music and the arts.

But what of man's frustration with his mind, that admirable organ superb at pattern recognition and intuitive, "fuzzy" logic but woefully slow at series calculations per second compared to modern computers and inaccurate in memory storage and recall. Computer technologies, as they embed both items of knowledge and portions of mental processes in outer devices, are a first step in man's effort to externalize powers of the mind and, ultimately, consciousness itself.

The primary importance of knowledge management, then, lies not in its benefits to business practice, scientific processes, or social efficiencies. The attempt to manage knowledge inevitably involves architectural questions not only about external knowledge structures, embedded or otherwise, but internal ones as well. The eventual blueprint that emerges for knowledge management may blur the line between external and internal knowledge, and thereby clarify it.

CONCLUSION

An entire consulting industry now lines up enthusiastically behind the banner, "Think outside the box." This dictum advises employees at all levels to consider options beyond the boundaries of ordinary workday paradigms. At Scandinavian Airlines, for example, virtually any employee with customer interface is empowered—usual policies notwithstanding—to work out a reasonable solution to complaints and service requests. But the empowerment and new energy that arises from such alternative paradigms for business comes at a price. "Thinking outside the box" means little if, puppy-like, we always have our "box" nearby to welcome us back from forays into the lesser known or unknown world.

The emerging science of knowledge management urges companies and those who run them to "get outside the box" or, more accurately, "forget about the box." In the same way that the zodiac and astrology cannot exist as co-partners and helpmates to the modern science of astronomy, so older "boxes" or paradigms of how business operates cannot remain unchanged by new approaches to managing and measuring knowledge.

"But that means," a manager could protest, "that I can't integrate knowledge management and measurement tools smoothly with my present operation." Correct! Paradigm shifts virtually never allow seamless transitions or long periods of problem-free integration. The rebels inevitably begin the revolution by killing the king. In the same way, the power of new ideas transform a company only when that firm is ready to leave the comfort zone of the "box" for the sake of growth, exploration, and even survival. Managing and measuring knowledge augurs an approach to business that, for all its short-term dislocations and discomforts, offers the long-term advantage of being more true.

QUESTIONS FOR REVIEW

1. What kinds of knowledge are more easily embedded in information technology? ·
2. What do you believe will be the pace of this embedding process?
3. What are the market implications for embedding knowledge?

4. What are the human resources implications for embedding more and more human knowledge in products and services?

5. How will this embedding process affect our ability to create new products and services over time?

6. What Darwinian processes are at work in the death of current management paradigms?

7. What is meta-knowledge and how will it set modern managers "free" in their quest for improving organizations?

8. Where do you believe knowledge management is headed in the near and far term as a new management approach?

APPENDIX: ANNOTATED BIBLIOGRAPHY

Bonner, Dede, ed. *In Action: Leading Knowledge Management and Learning.* Alexandria, VA: American Society for Training & Development, 2000.

Bukowitz, Wendi R., and Rutin L. Williams. *Knowledge Management Fieldbook.* Upper Saddle River, NJ: Financial Times Prentice Hall Printing, 1999.

Fischer, Layna. *Excellence in Practice.* Volume III: *Innovation & Excellence in Workflow Process and Knowledge Management.* New York: Future Strategies, 2000.

Frid, Randy J. *Infrastructure for Knowledge Management.* Lincoln, NE: IUniverse.com, 2000.

Hubert, Cindy, and Susan Elliot and Carla O'Dell. *Knowledge Management: A Guide for Your Journey to Best-Practice Processes.* Houston: APCQ Press.

Liebowitz, Jay. *Knowledge Management Handbook.* New York: CRC Press, 1999.

Malhotra, Yogesha. *Knowledge Management and Virtual Organizations.* Hershey, PA: Idea Group Publishing, 2000.

Organization for Economic Co-operation and Development. *Knowledge Management in the Learning Society.* Geneva, Switzerland: OECD, 2000.

Probst, Gilbert; Steffen Raub; and Kai Romhardt. *Managing Knowledge: Building Blocks for Success.* New York: John Wiley & Sons, 1999.

Schwartz, David; Monica Divitini; and Terie Brasethvik. *Internet-Based Organizational Memory and Knowledge Management.* Hershey, PA: Idea Group Publishing, 2000.

Tannenbaum, Scott I., and George M. Alliger. *Knowledge Management: Clarifying the Key Issues.* Chicago: IHRIM, 2000.

Thieraut, Robert. *Knowledge Management Systems for Business.* Westport, CT: Quorum Books, 1999.

Tiwana, Amrit. *The Knowledge Management Toolkit: Practical Techniques for Building a Knowledge Management System.* Upper Saddle River, NJ: Prentice Hall, 1999.

Bonner, Dede, ed. *In Action: Leading Knowledge Management and Learning.* Alexandria, VA: American Society for Training & Development, 2000.

Workplace learning and performance professionals stand poised to help create knowledge-friendly workplaces, where a mindset of continuous learning stimulates employee performance and replaces the old paradigm of training. Large and small companies worldwide are creating the position of chief knowledge officer or chief learning officer to design, develop, and coordinate new knowledge management and organizational learning initiatives. Read the 17 cases to get the real-life lessons learned from pioneer organizations and individuals who have already put knowledge management into practice to stay competitively vibrant.

Bukowitz, Wendi R., and Rutin L. Williams. *Knowledge Management Fieldbook.* Upper Saddle River, NJ: Financial Times Prentice Hall Printing, 1999.

This text provides the tools and techniques to set up, manage, and exploit a knowledge management system within your organization. It presents a comprehensive and practical approach to knowledge management.

Fischer, Layna. *Excellence in Practice.* Volume III: *Innovation & Excellence in Workflow Process and Knowledge Management.* New York: Future Strategies, 2000.

Frid, Randy J. *Infrastructure for Knowledge Management.* Lincoln, NE: IUniverse.com, 2000.

This book bridges the gap between the new demands being placed upon management and the tools used by information technology specialists in their attempt to manage information. It takes a look at both the cultural components required as well as the technology we can use to support knowledge capture and transfer.

Hubert, Cindy, and Susan Elliot and Carla O'Dell. *Knowledge Management: A Guide for Your Journey to Best-Practice Processes.* Houston: APCQ Press, 1998.

Based on years of research examining leading-edge organizations—and supported by examples of best practices and tips from actual practitioners—this book will guide readers through their own knowledge management endeavors. It provides mechanisms to gauge current status, understanding the components of a successful knowledge management initiative, and determine how to proceed.

Liebowitz, Jay. *Knowledge Management Handbook.* New York: CRC Press, 1999.

Integrates perspectives from researchers and practitioners on knowledge management and outlines a sound foundation of the methodologies, techniques, and practices within this field.

Malhotra, Yogesha. *Knowledge Management and Virtual Organizations.* Hershey, PA: Idea Group Publishing, 2000.

The focus is on understanding how knowledge creation, knowledge sharing, knowledge acquisition, knowledge exchange, knowledge transfer, and management of related risks can be understood and applied in the case of new organization forms including virtual web, virtual corporations, net broker, and business networks.

Organization for Economic Co-operation and Development. *Knowledge Management in the Learning Society*. Geneva, Switzerland: OECD, 2000.

It is increasingly important for companies and organizations to produce, share, and use knowledge on a national and global scale. However, little is known on how sectors and organizations could use knowledge more efficiently and how to benchmark organizations as learning organizations. This book attempts to address these issues through a better understanding of knowledge and learning processes at a sectorial level. It analyzes and compares the processes of knowledge production, dissemination, and use in engineering, information and communication technology, health, and education sectors.

Probst, Gilbert; Steffen Raub; and Kai Romhardt. *Managing Knowledge: Building Blocks for Success*. New York: John Wiley & Sons, 1999.

This book takes a "building block" approach to knowledge management. This structural approach results in a practical tool for analyzing the entire range of knowledge-related activities in an organization. Focused and well structured, this book helps managers better understand the many complexities of knowledge management and provides guidelines for charting a path forward.

Schwartz, David; Monica Divitini; and Terie Brasethvik. *Internet-Based Organizational Memory and Knowledge Management*. Hershey, PA: Idea Group Publishing, 2000.

The advent of the Internet as a fundamental infrastructure for the delivery of advanced business systems has opened up a wide range of questions for the design and development of such systems. Using the Internet as the primary architectural base, this book presents results and challenges of Internet-based knowledge management systems.

Tannenbaum, Scott I., and George M. Alliger. *Knowledge Management: Clarifying the Key Issues*. Chicago: IHRIM, 2000.

Knowledge management experts Scott Tannenbaum and George Alliger authored a collection of *IHRIM Journal* columns on the subject. These columns were adapted and restructured to create an all-inclusive knowledge management primer, *Knowledge Management: Clarifying the Key Issues*. The book raises questions, highlights potential pitfalls, and generates ideas for stimulating the application of knowledge to address organizational needs.

Thieraut, Robert. *Knowledge Management Systems for Business*. Westport, CT: Quorum Books, 1999.

Knowledge management systems can be used as a source of power to outmaneuver business competitors. Knowledge discovery tools enable decision makers to extract the patterns, trends, and correlations that underlie the inner (and inter-) workers of a company.

Tiwana, Amrit. *The Knowledge Management Toolkit: Practical Techniques for Building a Knowledge Management System*. Upper Saddle River, NJ: Prentice Hall, 1999.

This book delivers hands-on techniques and tools for making knowledge management happen at your company. It presents KM case studies from leading companies worldwide, from Nortel to Rolls Royce.

INDEX

A. D. Little, 65
Access management services, 115
Activity-based costing, 37–38
Affaers-vaerlden, 71
Age of the Spiritual Machine (Kurzweil), 152
Aggregate-level KVA, 97–102
Agro, 72
Allee, Verna, 79n, 131, 133, 134–135, 141
Amazon.com, 135, 142
American Express, 18
American Productivity and Quality Center, 59
Amoco, 46
Analog Devices, 71
Angus, Jeff, 12n
Apple Computer, 24
APQC, 25
Arthur, Brian, 30n, 79n
Arthur Andersen, 57, 59
Artificial intelligence, 3, 9, 57
Artificial knowledge, 2
Assets, 23
Astra-Draco, 74
AT&T, 22
Autonomy KnowledgeServer, 119

Baan, 56
Balanced scorecard approach, 38–39
Bank of America, 11
Baumard, Philippe, 74
Benetton, 72
Bethlehem Steel, 40
BMW, 149

Boeing 777, 71
Boeing Aircraft, 81, 146
Book value, 40
Booz Allen and Hamilton, 48
Bose CD player, 149
British Airways, 96
British Petroleum, 65, 73
    case, 69–70
Browning, Robert, 148
Buckman Labs, 71
Bureau of Labor Statistics, 21
Business intelligence services, 116
Business knowledge, 1
Business Process Engineering, 11
Business realities, 22

Canadian Imperial Bank of Commerce, 65
    case, 68–69
Carendi, Jan, 67
Carnegie Mellon University, 123
CBPO, 56
Celemi, 73
Celsius Tech, 74
Central knowledge organizations, 136–137
Chaparral Steel, 65, 71
    case, 69
Chase, R., 16n
Chase, Richard B., 51
Chase, Rory, 64n
Chase Manhattan, 18, 65
    case, 68–69
Chevron, 47, 65, 73
    case, 69
Chrysler Corporation, 46

Cisco Systems, 17, 135, 146
Clarke, Arthur C., 150
Coca-Cola Company, 24
Collaboration services, 113
Columbia/HCA Healthcare, 46
Communication services, 113
Company interfaces, 51–55
Compaq Computer, 27
Competition, 97
Competitive advantage, 7, 8–9
    of knowledge management, 49
Competitive environment, 16–17
Complexity, 39n
Computational tools, 110–111
Consumers, and knowledge metrics, 80–81
Core competencies, 68–69
Core services, 114–116
Cost approach, 83
Crick, Francis, 7
Customer errors, 51
Customer interface, 53
Customer knowledge, 50–55
Customer-knowledge-embedding principle, 50, 53–54
Customer relationship management, 116, 137–141
    steps, 140–141

Data communications, 19
Davenport, Thomas, 39
Da Vinci, Leonardo, 148
Dedijer, Steven, 74
Dell, Michael, 27

159

Dell Computer Corporation, 135
  case, 27–28
Delphi Consulting Group survey, 63–64
Department of Labor, 21
Deregulation; see Global deregulation
Digital library, 123–125
Distance learning, case, 61–62
Documentum Inc., 70
Documentum 4i software, 118–119
Dow Chemical, 46, 47, 73
  case, 65–66
Downsizing, risks in, 25, 79
Draper, S. W., 51n

eBay, 135
Economic value-added, 34
Economies in transition, 17–20
E-customer relationship management,
  137–141
Edvinsson, Leif, 34n, 67–68
Einstein, Albert, 7, 45
Electronic Data Systems, 23
Electronic economy, 16
Electronic marketplace, 17
Electronic propinquity, 128
Eli Lilly, 23
Elliot, R. K., 30n, 40n, 77n
Elliott, Susan, 25n
Ellison, Larry, 22
Embedded environment, 149
Embedded knowledge, 56, 59
  era of, 144
  limitations of, 146–148
  and meta-knowledge, 151
  omnipresent, 145
  paradigm failure, 147–148
  and technology, 148–149
  versus unembedded knowledge,
    146–147
Enterprise information portals, 116
Enterprise knowledge sharing systems,
  137
Enterprise resource planning software, 56
Enterprise Strategist, 58
e-Poke-Yoke notion, 51
Ericsson Radio, 74
Ernst & Young, 48, 57, 64
Ethernet, 24
eToys, 142
European Union, 20
Event horizon, 3
Excess earnings approach, 83
Exodus Communications, case, 95–106
Expansion of opportunity, 97
Extant knowledge, 9
Extranets, 19, 114

Fad Tracker, 58n

Fail-safeing principle, 54–55
First/best/least philosophy, 8
Ford Motor Company, 46, 71
Forest, William, 75–76
Fortune 500, 1
Freedom, 150–151
Freemasons, 8
Freud, Sigmund, 147–148
Frito-Lay, 72
Fruit of the Loom, 46

Galileo, 147
Gambro, 74
Gates, Bill, 22, 31
General Electric, 11, 65, 72, 135
General Motors, 46
Global deregulation, 19, 22
Global markets, 17–20
Greenspan, Alan, 78
Gross Domestic Product, 20
Groupware, 57

Handel, G. W., 7
Hawking, Stephen, 7
Hawthorne effect, 63
Helm, Leslie, 78n
Hewlett-Packard, 56, 65, 71
  case, 68
Hibbard, Justin, 70n
Holomapping technique, 133
Hom, Sandra, 16n
Home Depot, 142
Honda Motors, 72
Housel, Thomas J., 16n, 22n, 30n, 39n,
  80n, 109n, 128n
HTML document, 112
Hughes Space and Communications, 65
  case, 43–44
Human cognition, 3
Hyper-competition, 22–23

IBM, 17, 22, 23, 73, 149
IDC, 46
Ideas, 2
Ideational constraints, 2
Idea-versus-theory dilemma, 3
Immanent knowledge, 9
Income approach, 83–85
Indexing, 115
Industrial Age assumptions, 30–32, 127
Industrial Age managers, 32
Industry
  competitive environment, 16–17
  mergers and acquisitions, 19
Information, 25–26
Information Age assumptions, 30–32, 127
  failure of, 131
Information Age managers, 32

Information systems companies, 22
Information technology
  exponential use of, 78
  in knowledge management, 55–57
Information Technology Association of
  America, 21
Information technology industry, 21–22
Information technology jobs, 21
Information Week, 12
Informedia Digital Library Project, case,
  123–125
INFOSYS Technologies Incorporated,
  136
Infrastructrure, 110
Infrastructure services, 113–114
Intangible assets, 23
  value in, 40
Intellectual capital measures, 34–36
Intelligent agents, 114
Intelligent Systems Technology, Inc.,
  58, 94
Interface agents, 114
Internet, 9, 10
  case, 27–28
  in knowledge economy, 24–25
Internet Protocol networks, 19
Internet telephony, 19
Intranet, 19, 114
Inventory caching, 137
Investors, and knowledge metrics, 81–82

J. C. Penney, 147
Jackson Structured Diagrams, 95n
Java, 116n
JD Edwards, 56
Johnson, Samuel, 148
Junarkar, Bipin, 70

Kanevsky, Valery, 16n, 30n, 39n, 80n
Kaplan, Karen, 19
Kelly, Kevin, 25
Knowing, 3
Knowing relationship, 145–146
Knowledge; see also Embedded
  knowledge
  birth of, 4–5
  categories of, 10–12
  compared to information, 25–26
  creative use of, 82
  death of, 5–7
  definition and scope of, 2
  as economic resource, 45
  immanent and extant, 9
  versus knowledge services, 110
  overexercised, 6–7
  ownership of, 7–9
  and paradigm shifts, 5–6
  storage of, 9–10

time-bound nature of, 3
unexercised, 6
unstructured, 111
Knowledge asset portfolios, 129–130
   gaps in, 130–131
Knowledge assets, 17
   benefits of merging, 18
   components of, 21
   lost by downsizing, 25
   maintaining, 59
   value versus costs of, 23
Knowledge-based economies, 20–26, 21
Knowledge-based implementations,
   131–136
Knowledge capital, 21–23
   measuring, 33–34
Knowledge Capital methodology, 24
Knowledge capture services, 115
Knowledge earnings, 33
Knowledge economy, 15
   growth phase of, 78
   Internet use, 24–25
   and knowledge metrics, 79–80
   threats to growth, 79–80
Knowledge-gap assessment, 58–59
Knowledge generation services, 115
Knowledge life cycle, 136
Knowledge management
   benefits to companies, 46–47
   case, 13–14
   challenges and opportunities, 16–17
   for competitive advantage, 8–9
   current applications, 63–74
   current challenge of, 1
   current state of, 48–49
   customer relationship, 137–141
   definitions of, 12
   fundamental assumptions, 29–32
   future of, 143
   guiding assumptions, 127
   implementation questions, 129–130
   importance of, 49–50
   KSS checklist, 117–121
   KSS matrix, 117–121
   major services provided by, 113
   management positions, 65, 66
   in new economy, 25–26
   overview, 46–47
   paradigm shift, 128
   perceived benefits, 65
   principles
      customer knowledge, 50–55
      information technology, 55–57
      monitoring and measurement, 57–60
   problem definition, 109–111
   for products/services, 15–16
   supply chain, 137–141
   Swedish companies, 74

timetable, 64
tools
   core services, 114–116
   infrastructure services, 113–114
   knowledge services, 112–113
   knowledge structure, 111–112
   packaged services, 116
   and value creation, 47–48
   value networks, 131–136
Knowledge management initiatives, 47
Knowledge management maturity
   model, 136–137
Knowledge measurement
   activity-based costing, 37–38
   approaches, 33
   balanced scorecard, 38–39
   KVA approach, 40–41, 42
   output focus, 39
   procedures, 57–60
   process of elimination, 33–34
   reporting model, 34–36
   and value, 39–41
Knowledge metrics, 77
   as aid to growth, 79–80
   and consumers, 80–81
   and investors, 81–82
   and management, 82
   versus traditional valuation, 86
Knowledge organization, 23–26, 115
Knowledge piracy, 8
Knowledge redundancy strategy, 56–57
Knowledge seeking, 143
Knowledge services, 109, 110, 112–113
Knowledge spawners, 4
Knowledge strategy, 142
Knowledge structure, 109, 111–112
Knowledge value added, 40–41, 42, 83
   aggregate-level, 97–102
   approaches to, 95
   case, 95–106
   fundamental assumptions, 94
   methodology, 91–93
   sales provisioning process, 102–106
Knowledge-value-added theory, 93–95
Kochikar, V. P., 136
Koulopoulos, Thomas, 24n
KSS checklist
   function, 117–118
   tools for using, 118–121
KSS matrix
   function, 117
   tools for using, 118–121
Kuhn, Thomas, 29, 30
Kurtyka, Jerry, 139n, 140
Kurzweil, Ray, 152
KVA; see Knowledge value added

L. L. Bean, 137

Label knowledge, 10–11
Learning-knowledge-value cycle,57–59,
   129
Leonard-Barton, Dorothy, 69
Lev, Baruch, 33
Lewis, C., 51n
Locked knowledge, 145
Logic, 2
Lotus Notes, 69, 70, 113
Lotus Notes R5, 120

Managers
   Information Age versus Industrial
      Age, 32
   and knowledge metrics, 82
   need for measurement, 32–41
Manasco, Britton, 43n
Marketing circle of life, 140–141
Market value, 24, 40
McDonald's, 1
MCI Communications, 25
McKesson, case, 87–89
McKinsey and Bain and Company, 73
McNealy, Scott G., 22
Measurement; see also Knowledge
   measurement
   essential to management, 32–41
   need for new methods, 30–31
   in science, 29
   traditional methods, 77, 82–86
Merck and Company, 23
Mergers and acquisitions, 19
Meta-knowledge, 150–151
Meta-knowledge management,
   151–153
Microsoft Corporation, 7, 22, 24, 31,
   32, 40
Microsoft Office, 116n
Microsoft Word, 115
Milton, John, 9
Monitoring, 57–60
Monsanto, 46, 65, 70
Montgomery Ward, 147
Moral philosophies, 2
Mozart, W.A., 148
My Yahoo!, 116

NASDAQ, 96
National Bicycle, 72
Nature
   and embedded knowledge, 148–149
   and technology, 149–150
NCR, 22
Neiser, Julian, 124n
NetBill, 124
Netscape Communications, 7–8, 72
Neural networks, 57
New business realities, 22

New economy
   knowledge management in, 25–26
   knowledge organization in, 23–26
Nordstrom, 96, 147
Norman, D., 51n
Nortel, 17
Nova Corporation, 56

O'Dell, Carla, 25
OpenText LiveLink, 119
Options theory, 86
Oracle, 22, 31, 56
Order fulfillment, 137–139
Organization for Economic Cooperation
   and Development, 20
Organizations
   benefits of knowledge management,
      46–47
   death of knowledge in, 5
   knowledge management maturity
      levels, 136–137
   knowledge management positions, 66
   market value, 24
   new business realities, 22
Oticon, 71
Outoku-mppu, 73

Packaged services, 116
Palo Alto Research Center, 24
Paradigms, 29
   birth and death of, 147–148
   measurement methods, 30–32
   underlying assumptions, 29–32
Paradigm shift, 5–6, 29, 128
Patel, Jeetu, 12n
Payne, Laurie, 44n, 70n
People knowledge, 11–12
PeopleSoft, 56, 116
PeopleSoft Customer Relationship
   Management, 121
Performance ratios, 59–60
Personal communication services, 22
Peterson, Jonathan, 78n
Picasso, Pablo, 149
Platt, Lew, 68
PLS-Consult, 72
PLX.com, 86
Poke-Yoke, 51
Price, Timothy, 25
Priceline.com, 96
Price-to-book value, 96n
Principle of replication, 94
Principles, 45
ProcessEdge, 94
Process knowledge, 11
Process of elimination approach, 33–34
Product/service, 15–16
Product/service redefinition, 80–81
Profit margin, 97

Proof, 2
Proprietary knowledge, 7–9
Prozac, 149
Prusak, Larry, 39

Railing, Larry, 128n
Real options approach, 86
Reengineering strategies, 48
Regional Bell Operating Company, 48
Relative distribution, 2
Relative usefulness, 2
Replication, 94
Retrieval services, 116
Return on investment, 81
Return on knowledge, 91–93, 94, 101,
   130
Return on process, 94
Ritz Carlton, 73
ROI; see Return on investment
ROK; see Return on knowledge
Rutledge, John, 23n, 34n

Saffo, Eric, 31
Sales provisioning process, 102–106
SAP, 31, 56
SBC Corporation, 93
Scandinavian Airline System, 74, 153
Scientific management, 30
Sears, 1, 142, 147
Seidenberg, Ivan, 25n
SGML, 112
Shakespeare, William, 7
Shannon, Claude, 30n, 40n, 80n
Siebel, 116
Silicon Graphics, 48
Sirbu, Marvin, 124
Skandia, 34n, 65, 74
   case, 67–68
Skilled workers, 21
Skill knowledge, 11
Skopec, Eric, 22n
Slaughter-Langdon, C., 79n
Stanton, Keith, 56n
Stata, Ray, 71
Steelcase, 48, 73
Stentor, 65
Stewart, Douglas M., 51n
Stewart, Thomas A., 21n, 23n, 37, 45n
Strassman, Paul A., 24, 33–34
Structure of Scientific Revolutions
   (Kuhn), 29
Sun Microsystems, 22
Supply chain, 138
Supply chain knowledge, 137–141
Sveiby, Karl Eric, 47, 73
Swedish Coalition of Service Industries,
   67
Swedish companies, 74
Systems map, 134–135

Tangible assets, 23
Tapscott, Don, 21n
Technological change, 19
Technological forest, 149–150
Technology
   and embedded environment, 149
   and embedded knowledge, 148–149
Telecommunications industry
   consolidation, 18–19
Teledesic, 22
Television technology, 8
Telia, 73, 74
3M Corporation, 71
Total quality management, 64
Translation services, 113

U. S. West
Unembedded knowledge, 146–147
United Radiology, case, 75–76
United States
   knowledge workers, 21
   mergers and acquisitions, 19
Unstructured knowledge, 111
USA Today, 96

Valente, Andre, 109n
Valuation, 2
   cost approach, 83–85
   income approach, 83–85
   market approach, 84–85
   real options approach, 86
   traditional methods, 82–86
Value and knowledge, 39–41
Value creation, 47–48
Value drivers, 81
Value exchange, 132–133, 135
Value Network Analysis, 135
Value Network Diagram, 134–135
Value networks, 131–136
Volvo, 74

Ward, Arian, 43–44
Watson, James, 7
Weather.com, 96
Wellsprings of Knowledge (Leonard-
   Barton), 69
Wireless services, 22
Wolrath, Bjorn, 67
Workflow management services, 113
World Bank, 65
   case, 67–68
World Com/MCI, 22
World Trade Organization, 20

Xerox Corporation, 24
Xerox New Enterprises, 24
XML, 112

Yahoo!, 96, 112